Party *of* One

Party *of* One

A MEMOIR IN 21 SONGS

Dave Holmes

CROWN
ARCHETYPE
NEW YORK

Library of Congress Cataloging-in-Publication Data
Names: Holmes, Dave, 1971–
Title: Party of one : a memoir in 21 songs / Dave Holmes.
Description: First edition. | New York : Crown Archetype, an imprint of the
    Crown Publishing Group, a division of Penguin Random House LLC,
    2016.
Identifiers: LCCN 2015047486 | ISBN 9780804187985 (hardback) | ISBN
    9780804188005 (electronic)
Subjects: LCSH: Holmes, Dave, 1971– | Holmes, Dave, 1971– —Childhood
    and youth. | Comedians—United States—Biography. | Television
    personalities—United States—Biography. | Radio personalities—
    United States—Biography. | Authors, American—Biography. | Gay
    men—United States—Biography. | Coming of age—United States.
    | Self-acceptance—United States. | Popular music—United States—
    Miscellanea. | BISAC: BIOGRAPHY & AUTOBIOGRAPHY /
    Personal Memoirs. | HUMOR / General. | MUSIC / Genres & Styles /
    Pop Vocal. Classification: LCC CT275.H6446 A3 2016 | DDC 780.92—
    dc23 LC record available at https://lccn.loc.gov/2015047486

ISBN 978-0-8041-8798-5
eBook ISBN 978-0-8041-8800-5

Printed in the United States of America

Book design by Lauren Dong
Jacket design by Jake Nicolella
Jacket artwork by

10 9 8 7 6 5 4 3 2 1

First Edition

To Dad, Mom, Dan, and Steve,
for messing me up the exact right amount.

[TRACK LISTING]

Life is about love, last minutes and lost evenings,
About fire in our bellies and about furtive little feelings,
And the aching amplitudes that set our needles all
  a-flickering,
They help us with remembering that the only thing
  that's left to do is live.

—FRANK TURNER,
  "I Knew Prufrock Before He Got Famous"

Intro

OF ALL THE EPIC STORIES, BOTH FACTUAL AND FIC-
tional, that we have passed down through history, I identify most strongly with the journey of the Bee Girl in Blind
Melon's "No Rain" video. If you didn't happen to spend your
life in front of a television in 1992, here's the situation: a
plucky, bespectacled girl, maybe nine years old, has dressed up
in a cheap bumblebee costume that looks like it was made by a
parent in a great big hurry—and all she wants to do is dance.
Throughout the video, Bee Girl tap-dances her little heart out,
giving everything she's got to everyone she meets, and over
and over she's met with stone faces. *Move it along,* the people
of the town seem to tell her as the song shambles on. Nobody
is interested, but does she give up? No, she does not. *I've got
spirit yes I do, I've got spirit, how about . . . you?* she wonders.
Are you *my people? Do I belong* here? No, no, and no.

And then, as the song reaches its post-*Nevermind,* pre–
Rusted Root, Woodstock '94–bound crescendo, Bee Girl
approaches the wrought-iron gate of a peaceful pasture, and
with a look of pure amazement and joy swings the gate open
to reveal a *whole field of frolicking bee-people.* Bee-people young
and old, black and white, each united by their unfortunate

costumes and love of dance. She is home. She has found her people. *There* you are, you imagine her saying with a sigh.

I remember seeing this video for the first time in college—miserable, half-drunk on Keystone Light, a Camel Light smoldering my mouth, about to desperately tap-dance my way through another social interaction—and saying out loud: "I fucking *get* you, Bee Girl."

My name's Dave Holmes, and I have spent most of my life being the odd man out. In retrospect the only negative part about that is how much time I spent thinking it was a bad thing.

I hunted high and low for my place in this world. I changed myself around every which way to make myself normal. I tried to be each of the five archetypes from *The Breakfast Club*, all four of the *Facts of Life* girls, every one of the emotions inside *Herman's Head*. I tore it *up*, you guys. It didn't work, exactly, but if my unquenchable thirst for acceptance sent me on a long series of wrong turns, I'm exactly where I want to be now. I'm not going to tell you that I found my field of frolicking bee-people inside me, because then I would have to close my laptop, fill my pockets with stones, and walk into the ocean. But if you find you're reaching that conclusion on your own, I'm not going to stand in your way.

I did a lot of embarrassing things and put myself through a lot of useless trouble on the road to accepting myself, and it would have been a much more painful experience had I not had access to the most powerful stimulant known to humankind: the music and popular culture of the last forty years. I came of age in the time of the Monoculture, when we were all watching the same three networks and listening to the same Top 40 radio stations. My identity was formed in the eras of *Thriller*, *The Cosby Show*, and Nirvana—all those stories ended well, right?—and when I felt like I didn't have a friend in the world, they were there for me. I had intense love affairs with albums. I saw movies so many times I could direct them from memory. I spent so much time in front of MTV it finally gave up and invited me in.

In my younger days, my preferred method of communication was a mixtape (and then a mix-CD, and then, ever so briefly, a mix-MiniDisc). I could tell people I liked them, or that I wanted them to like me, or that I was breaking up with them, or that I understood they were breaking up with me (but if they could just understand how I felt, maybe they'd change their minds) in ninety minutes of music. It's the way a nonmusician could make his own album, the way a kid too scared to speak his mind could get his point across.

It's still my favorite thing to do, and you better believe I tried to sell my publisher on getting this into the marketplace as an Apple Music playlist, but these book types insist that you use words. So here they are: stories of the blessed and stupid life of a kid on the margins, and the music that moved it forward, in book form, which I figured I should hurry up and do before we start passing down our histories via emojis and GIFs of Rue McClanahan. I put it together like an album, with a few interludes in between, like how hip-hop albums used to have skits. (But, you know, maybe they'll age better.)

I hope you like it. I hope I bring back some memories or help you understand a beautiful time in recent history that is absolutely gone forever. And if you are in the middle of your own desperate tap-dance right now, I hope that you can learn from my mistakes.

Just stay with me, and we'll have it made.

1

Go Your Own Way

I PLAYED FOR THE ST. GERARD'S FIRST-GRADE BOYS'
soccer team because participation was compulsory, sports
were a thing a boy was expected to take to, and I liked being
where the boys were besides. They'd put me at goalie, which
was a smart tactical move because I wasn't very good at the
running or the kicking or the remembering which way to go
when I had the ball. I wasn't *into* it. All the bewildering action
was happening a world away in midfield, and I'd already done
the thing where I tangled myself up in the net and pretended I
was a Spider-Man villain; my work in the game felt done. And
there was an audience *right there:* a bleacher full of parents and
siblings, some from St. G's, some from the opposing parish,
Mary Queen of Peace—a crowd, I imagined, as starved for
entertainment as I was. I knew where I was needed.

I walked over to the bleachers and shook some hands.
"Good to see you, Mr. and Mrs. Gunn. Is that a new blouse,
Mrs. Edwards? Lovely." I could hear Coach O'Connor calling
me back to my post, but I had put myself where I knew I could
do the most good. "Can that be *Angela*, Mrs. DiNunzio? *No.*
She's growing up *too fast*." My parents tried to get my attention and point me toward the field. "Let's do a cheer," I told
my public. "How about 'This Team Is Red Hot'—Do we all

know that one? I'll start." The parents from Mary Queen of Peace got louder and louder, until they broke out into full applause and stood—which felt premature, given that I hadn't even gotten into my impressions yet—but the ovation was not for me. I turned around just in time to see that one of their kids had sent the ball right into my untended goal. I clapped and whooped along with them; *Scoring is good no matter who does it,* I figured. *It's why we're here in the first place.* A few of the parents began to laugh, and I was too young to know it was *at me.* I just knew I was getting a reaction, and a reaction felt good. I'd never felt like I had much to offer out on the field, but this, *this,* was something I could do.

Coach O'Connor was a patient man, but he had his limits. "Hey, Holmes?" he called out to me, "isn't there somewhere you should be?"

Of course there was. I turned back to the bleachers: "Is anybody celebrating an *anniversary*?"

+   +   +

My family's game was well in progress by the time I made it to the field—my parents had my brothers, Dan and Steve, a year and a half apart, and then exactly eight years later, me— so entertaining from the sidelines has always been my default position. Those who can neither do nor teach have a tendency to observe and make jokes.

Like any good St. Louis family, my family loves sports. They aren't obsessed—they don't wear jerseys or paint their torsos or perform strange rituals beyond some enthusiastic marching in place to the Notre Dame fight song—but they're into it. We had season tickets to the football Cardinals in the years before the owner moved them to wherever they are now—boy, was that the talk of the town that I sort of half listened to—and while I loved going along, I never paid a bit of attention to the game. Who could, when there was so much else going on? When you could analyze the cheerleaders and try to determine which was the one the rest of them didn't like? When the guy three rows ahead of you with the huge pink face got drunker and drunker on the ice-cold beers the vendor kept selling him, and his wife silently planned her escape? When you were scanning the audience for someone else who was looking at the world the same way you were, who also called the crowd at a football game an "audience"? Life was unfolding all around—who cared which team got the most points?

My family is also Catholic, which meant that we showed up at 11:00 Mass every Sunday, with breakfast at the IHOP after. Catholicism is supposed to contain and explain all the mysteries of an infinite universe, but you're not supposed to ask questions. You're supposed to sing along with the hymns, but not too loudly. You're supposed to sit—and stand, and kneel, and genuflect—quietly in church, and if that's hard for you to do, you're supposed to give it as an offering to Our Lord Jesus Christ. (*Affer it up t'Are Lard*, Mom would whisper to us; you're evidently also supposed to know what that means.) You're expected to worship an invisible, unknowable being who made the whole world in six days and then rested for one, who sent his only son to die on a cross because of what you did or might someday do or might someday *think* about doing, all so that someday you can go live on a cloud with them and all your dead relatives and favorite celebrities for an infinite number of forevers. But you're not supposed to be weird about it. When your main objective is to be a good kid, Catholicism makes everything extremely complicated.

Growing up, my brothers stood as two ball-playing, Catholic-etiquette-understanding examples of what boys were supposed to be. They were effortlessly athletic and personable, smart and charismatic. They were *cool*. Dan was in a Catholic high school in Midtown St. Louis that had a military option, which he chose voluntarily, in classic oldest-child fashion. Steve went to a different one in the suburbs with a good football program. Dan could do all kinds of drills with his rifle; he could tap me on the shoulders with the Wiffle-ball bat from the garage and make me a knight like he saw in Camelot. Steve could do all the Muppets' voices and throw a tennis ball so high in the air it became a tiny speck and then I couldn't even see it anymore. And I begged them to do it all again and again. It was the best show in town.

Where they could wrestle or race each other and be more or less evenly matched, either one of them could demolish me so easily there was no point in my even trying. When they tossed a baseball at each other, it would make that satisfying, forceful little *pop* when it would hit the other's glove; my throws would make a sad little arc ending halfway to my intended target, an average of thirty degrees to the left. They knew how to talk to and win over kids their age; I gave up on my peers when I couldn't find anyone who wanted to discuss *Mary Hartman, Mary Hartman*.

They were also skilled at the art of being good older brothers. It's Steve who taught me how to read, when he was ten and I was two. We watched *Sesame Street* together, and after each episode he'd make flash cards to reinforce the lessons of the day. Because it meant more time together, I'd go over them again and again until I was reading whole sentences. I became a local celebrity: The Kid Who Can Read. I'd read the slogan of the local dry cleaner out loud—"If we can't clean it, it can't be cleaned"—and follow along with Father Shea from the missalette during Mass. If I didn't understand what I was saying, I knew how people were reacting. They noticed me, and I liked being noticed. So I kept doing it, and by the time I was in first grade, I was reading way beyond my grade level. I promise I'm not bragging here; the reason two-year-olds tend not to read is that people tend not to teach them. It's one of the pillars of Montessori education: you can pretty much teach a kid anything anytime; once he picks up a new skill, he tends to keep doing it until he gets really good.

The problem is that I didn't go to a Montessori school. Here's what happens when you show up for first grade at a Catholic parish school reading way beyond your grade level:

When it came time for first grade reading, Miss Streibel would stop everything and call out into the hallway for a massive teacher-in-training named Gary, who would take my hand in his sweaty palm and lead me to the priests' lounge just off the gymnasium for one-on-one reading time. (I know where your mind is going. Relax.)

First grade reading coincided with sixth grade PE, and if there's anything sixth-graders for sure do not like, it's a younger child who can do something they can't. So when Gary and I entered the gym for the long walk to the priests' lounge, we would immediately be pelted with whatever the sixth-graders were playing with: dodgeballs, basketballs, or, if they were just running sprints, their actual shoes. The gym teacher would blow her whistle, but it would be in vain; the people had spoken. This went on for weeks.

Like Markie Post in a Lifetime Original Movie, I kept my abuse to myself. I swore Gary to secrecy about the whole thing, and I made eye contact with the gym teacher as if to say: It's fine, I'm asking for it. But the principal got wind of our problem and came up with a solution only a Catholic educator could love: for the rest of the school year, when Gary and I would enter the gym, the sixth-graders were forced to stop what they were doing—right in the middle of whatever game they were playing—and sit on the floor in silence with their hands folded in their laps as we walked the endless perimeter to the priests' lounge. I can say this with a certainty that is hard-won: silent glares sting the face worse than dodgeballs.

But then I'd go home, and I'd read something for my parents, and I'd see how proud it made them, and I'd feel right in the world again. Being an early reader alienated me at school, but at home, I was safe.

I was different, and they liked me that way.

＊　＊　＊

My folks pulled me out of St. Gerard's after first grade, and during that between-schools summer, I did a lot of thinking about my former classmates. A lot of them I'd be seeing around the neighborhood or at Mass, but there was one who I wasn't sure I'd ever see again, and I was surprised by how sad the thought of it made me. His name was Donny, and he was an athletic, confident kid who seemed to just move correctly: chest out, shoulders back, stride confident. He was the first picked at soccer, always. When we were at recess and trying to decide what to play, everyone naturally glanced over at him for guidance. He was a real boy. I wanted to be him, or be near him, or just have him put his arm around me. I didn't know. I didn't care.

I just thought: *We need to get that kid over here.*

And so one June morning, as my family gathered around the kitchen table for bacon and eggs, I asked my mom to call his mom and see if he'd want to come over. "It would be fun to hang around," I told her. "I want to keep in touch with him."

"Huh," Mom said. "I didn't know you and Donny were such good friends."

"Oh, we're not," I told her. "I just think he's cute."

And the pause button was hit on the entire world.

Everyone and everything froze. I had stopped time. If this had happened in a movie trailer, we all would have heard a record scratch and our dog would have covered his eyes.

In that moment, I knew that I had done something that was a special kind of wrong. I hadn't hurt anyone, I hadn't lied, I hadn't sworn or littered or taken Are Lard's name in vain, I had done something worse. I knew it because I couldn't even figure out what it was. I knew it because nobody knew how to react. We were all in new territory.

My mother spoke first: "So, when you say that you think Donny is cute"—she wasn't angry, she was dazed, as if from a punch to the face—"do you mean that you think he's handsome? Or do you mean something else, like he says cute things and he's funny and that's why you like him?"

It was clear which choice would make the world start spinning again.

"The second one. The cute things he says. He's always saying funny things. He's so funny." He wasn't all that funny.

"Okay," she said. Relieved. A weight lifted. The air in the room began to circulate again. "Okay, hon. When that's what you mean, you should say a boy is *funny*. Boys don't call other boys *cute.*" The message was delivered with love, but she looked me right in the eyes to make sure it was delivered. She was just trying to protect me, I can see that now.

Different means unique and distinct, but in St. Louis in the 1970s, if you changed the tone up just a little bit, the word became an insult. People in the Midwest are kind to one another, so they won't say someone is too loud or too quiet or thick in the head or light in the loafers, they'll just say: "That kid is *different.*" It can mean a lot of things, and you don't want to be any of them.

I remember this moment, because it is when I split into two pieces. It was the moment I realized that there would be a self that I could show the world and a self I'd have to keep hidden. If I wanted to be acceptable, if I wanted to spare myself and my family the shame of being *different,* I'd have to do some work.

I didn't think about it again for a very long time, but it left behind an ache.

The drug I numbed myself with was the radio. The song we sang along to the most that summer was Billy Joel's "Just the Way You Are."

There's a reason why gay men have a finely tuned sense of irony.

2

Hungry Heart

ERE'S A FUN FACT: BEFORE IT BECAME ANOTHER OF America's numerous occasions for large groups of young adults to sleep with and/or spit up on one another, Halloween was a popular holiday among children. In St. Louis in the 1970s, the culture had yet to embrace adult cosplay or the concept that kittens could be made sexy; October 31 was a time for kids to collect fistfuls of fun-size Milky Way bars, thank their elders, and nothing more.

Candy notwithstanding, it wasn't all that hot a holiday for kids, either. If you wanted to go as, say, C-3PO—as I did for three perfectly adequate years in a row—that meant your parents' going to the drugstore and buying a $4 box that included a plastic suffocation hazard of a mask sprayed with carcinogenic gold paint, to be worn atop a vomit-repelling synthetic poncho carrying a fresco of scenes from *Star Wars*. One would go more as *the idea of C-3PO* than the droid himself. This didn't satisfy my need for self-expression, so to amp up the realness, I would totter stiffly between houses, robot arms at perfect 90-degree angles, which would slow, and annoy, my neighborhood trick-or-treat group (and reduce my overall candy haul)—but I like to commit to a performance.

By the time I hit third grade, I was ready to take ownership of my Halloween experience. Since I'd seen some on television, by mid-September I had made the firm decision that for Halloween 1980, I would be a punk rocker. There was plenty of room for interpretation here; to anyone who wasn't a coastal teenager at the turn of the decade, "punk rock" was a catch-all term for "anything you didn't often see." Sort of spiky hair: punk. Those plastic sunglasses that were essentially one long narrow lens: *very* punk. One Specials button on an otherwise pristine denim jacket: Mister, you might as well be GG Allin. I began silently taking an inventory of clothing and household items I could use: Could I tear up an old pair of jeans? Snip a sleeve off a shirt? Cut a head hole in a trash bag and cinch it at the waist with a bike lock? My mind reeled with the possibilities, with the danger and responsibility that making a bold personal statement entails. I decided I'd show my family when the whole costume was thoroughly workshopped and realized.

I went down the street to my friend Molly's house for dinner later that week and told her family of my tentative trick-or-treating plans. Her mom sprang up; "I have just the thing," she said, and then disappeared into her bedroom, emerging moments later with a silver-sequined pantsuit and its own matching beret. "I never wear it anymore. It's yours. You can cut it up however you like." I thought: *Yes. Yes, that's exactly what I'm going to do.* I walked that pantsuit back home, snuck it up to my room, used my safety scissors to alter the arms and legs to my size, and chose the perfect dangerous angle at which to wear the beret. After dinner the next night, I gathered my parents and brothers in the living room to model my creation.

Have you ever confused a Jack Russell terrier, to the point where it looks concerned and cocks its head at a 45-degree angle? Then you have seen what each member of my family looked like when I walked into our living room.

My oldest brother, Dan, could not find words. My middle brother, Steve, a senior in high school, said, "You know, Dave," and after a moment or two of searching for the right thing to tell me, "that's not really what punk rock is," as though strict costume interpretation were the primary concern when your eight-year-old brother stands before you in a silver-sequined ladies' pantsuit and matching beret.

My reply—I swear to God—was this: "But I can do the splits, like Mick Jagger. Watch!"

Okay. Here are a few of the flaws in this argument:

1. Mick Jagger could not do the splits.
2. The splits are not generally considered a punk-rock move.
3. Mick Jagger is not generally considered a punk rocker.
4. I also could not do the splits.

I rose from the ground, having attempted the splits and succeeded at nothing more than testing the tensile strength of the pantsuit's base fabric, but I was triumphant. I was agile and dangerous. I was a punk rocker. It was immediately clear to my family that I would not be deterred, and I guess everyone agreed that there were some lessons I should learn the hard way.

A solid 70 percent of houses guessed that I was dressed as a fancy pimp. Whatever—I still got candy. Molly went as a calculator.

So, anyway, that was the Halloween I dressed as A Source of Concern to My Family.

*   *   *

They need not have worried, really. I come by my exuberance for music and popular culture naturally; it's the primary thing I inherited from my family. There is nothing that you can say to either of my parents that won't remind them of a song, and they will never fail to sing it. My point is not that they'll break into "You Are The Sunshine of My Life" when you tell them it's sunny outside, or "The Way We Were" when you mention something that has happened in the past, although these are absolutely things that will happen. What I'm saying is that literally everything—airplane tickets, Styrofoam, the flu—is a cue for a song, and it is always time to be singing. They're like improv performers, just waiting for a suggestion so they can launch into their act. We're Irish; it can't be helped.

My father worked as a financial consultant of some sort; throughout my youth, he put on a tie and managed money and didn't talk much about it when he got home. But he made a point of taking us to New York once a year, and when we were there he made sure to get Broadway tickets for at least three nights. He'd slip the concierge a few bucks for the really good seats, so we'd be always right up in front. (Except at *Cats*, whose good seats are in the first row of the balcony, where the cat chorus crawls right up next to you and rubs their heads on your chest and purrs and you silently wish you had slightly worse seats.) Dad would get lost in the show. I could see the whites of his eyes in the dark of the theater. And after the final number, he would stand. He would *whoop*. There would be tears in his eyes sometimes, even if it wasn't a very good show. He'd been transported. He and my mother have been married since the early 1950s, when every suburban home had the

Original Cast Recordings of *West Side Story, The King And I, The Sound of Music*. My dad had a secret identity as a theater buff.

My mother grew up in North St. Louis, a Sinatra-worshipping bobby-soxer from way back, who wrote letters to Frank offering her babysitting services for Frank Jr. and Nancy. Any time my parents travel, my mother sees celebrities. It's uncanny. They will come back from a trip and she'll pull a list of names and quick first impressions out of her purse. "Marion Ross: nice as can be. Gavin MacLeod: seems impressed with himself. Sandy Duncan: no bigger than a minute." Sometime in the '90s when my folks visited me in New York, Mom came back from a shopping trip a little out of breath but exhilarated. "I saw Hugh Grant at FAO Schwarz and I followed him all the way down Fifth Avenue," she told me. "And your thoughts?" "I'm not sure I trust him," she confided. "It seemed like he was trying to hide from someone." That it will absolutely never occur to my mother that Hugh Grant might have been trying to give *her* the slip is part of her charm. (It's also possible that she's just a shrewd judge of character; the Divine Brown thing was only a few months ahead.) She's a magnet for boldface names, in a way that might qualify as an actual medical condition. Recently, Steve and his wife, Betsy, went on a last-minute ski vacation, and with no time to shop for her own, Betsy borrowed my mother's ski vest. The first ski lift they got on, their seatmate was golfer Phil Mickelson. Steve and Betsy looked at each other and said the same thing: "It's a *pheromone*."

Loving entertainment was the only thing I could do as well as everyone else in the house. When I was little and my brothers were still home, the car radio was always on the Top

40 AM radio station, and everybody sang along. If I couldn't throw a ball the way my brothers could, if I couldn't keep up with my parents' conversation, when the radio was on we were all on the same page in the same songbook. *Nothing from nothing leaves nothing. Rock the boat, don't tip the boat over. Jet, I thought that the major was a lady.* I didn't understand a word I was singing and it didn't matter; I was doing the same thing my family was doing, and it felt good. (Years later, I told Kurt Loder about this, about how the music of Paul McCartney and Wings was the first thing that made me feel connected to the world, and his immediate reply was: "Did it bother you that Paul McCartney and Wings were *awful?*" Kurt Loder is Kurt Loder all day long.)

Like pretty much everyone in my generation whose home had electricity, I also spent hours sitting directly in front of the television. For the youth of the era, turn-of-the-decade Saturday nights were all about the ABC lineup: *The Love Boat* and, for those whose parents allowed it, *Fantasy Island* (Mr. Roarke got a little hard-PG with those fantasies sometimes). On Tuesdays, it was *Charlie's Angels,* which I would watch with my mother. At the beginning of each episode, when the Angels gathered to talk to the squawk box on the desk, my mother would say the same thing, in the same way: "That's *John Forsythe,*" she'd tell me, and then, in a whisper: *"He's quite handsome."* My immediate impression was that he was simply *too* handsome to be on camera; that if he were to show his face, the female viewers of *Charlie's Angels* would pass out with hearts in their eyes like lovestruck young kittens in a Heckle & Jeckle cartoon and miss the show so many people had worked so hard to make. (I would go on to remain fully conscious when John

Forsythe starred as Blake Carrington in *Dynasty*. He was all right. Settle down, Mom.)

I also developed a taste for daytime television. One Christmas break, I caught my mother watching *All My Children* as she ironed Dad's shirts. It was her secret habit, and I sensed her shame at having become the kind of woman who watched soap operas. I mildly gave her the business at first—*"Really, Mom? Love in the afternoon?"* But by day two I was starting to recognize faces and names, and then I was starting to actively wonder why Erica and Brooke didn't get along, or why Greg's mom didn't like Jenny, and Mom furnished the backstories. By the end of Christmas break I was teaching her how to program the VCR so that I could watch it after school. She quit cold turkey shortly thereafter; I stuck with it right up to the bitter end.

And I mean *bitter:* the show ended its four-decade-plus network run on a cliffhanger in which a drunk and rageful J.R. shot blindly into a party. *Who did J.R. shoot?* was the question they intended to leave us with, hoping we'd forget that at least a third of the guests at this party had already died on camera. Some had actually returned as ghosts for holiday episodes, or donated organs to other characters who were also at that party, but somehow they had been found in the basement of Dr. David Hayward, who had been keeping them alive this whole time—even the ones who had died when he would have been, like, eleven years old. Who cares who gets shot when there's a guy in town who can *cure death?* (You guys, I might still be holding on to some anger and frustration about the way *All My Children* ended.)

But I was drawn mostly to music, and my brothers' peak

record-buying years happened to produce the kind of music a younger brother would most want to borrow. Dan was into what at the time was called AOR—Kansas and Foghat and that "Iron Man" song by Black Sabbath that sent me screaming to my room to hide in the closet, because it was legitimately scary to a child, and also I was too young to recognize when I was actually living out a metaphor. Dan's albums had gatefold sleeves and intricate artwork: Queen's *News of the World* cover depicted a giant robot unwittingly wreaking havoc on a city, holding the dead, bloodied band in his cold, steel palm, thinking: *What have I done? Led Zeppelin IV* had mystical symbols and an old man carrying a massive bundle of sticks on his back, and only the teenagers seemed to know what it all meant. (St. Louis's radio tastes froze at right around this time in history; when I go back to visit, everyone still seems to listen to KSHE-95, the classic rock station. It used to bother me, but coming home and hearing Rush's "Tom Sawyer" within thirty minutes of my arrival brings order and stability to the world.)

Steve was into Magic 108, the soul music station. There are a few classic albums from this period in R&B: *Off the Wall, Songs in the Key of Life,* The Brothers Johnson's *Blam!,* but it's mostly about the singles: Ray, Goodman & Brown's "Special Lady." Cheryl Lynn's "Got to Be Real," Shalamar's "Second Time Around." Larry Graham's "One in a Million You." Dan and Steve's stereos fought with each other every night until lights out at 10:00—dance beats and quiet storm ballads on one side, brainy lyrics and heavy guitars on the other. Right in the middle was the place to be.

The one thing they could agree on musically was Bruce

Springsteen, who was revered by both as a god living among us. They each had their own copy of every one of his albums, from *Greetings from Asbury Park, NJ* right up to *The River.* They also pooled their money on a tape player for the Buick Wildcat convertible they shared so that they could each buy all of his albums on 8-track. I begged to tag along on their errands, where we'd sing along to "She's the One," and it would fade out in the middle, click, and fade back up. Errands are a major event for a kid with cool big brothers.

Each day, I became more aware that I was both different and *different*, and each day, I turned to music to ease the discomfort. I was insatiable; I took from my brothers, but I had to have more. Outside the family, my most reliable ally around these times was Casey Kasem. For Christmas 1980, I got roller skates—red Nike numbers that looked like sneakers with big red wheels on them. And each Sunday morning, I woke up early, pulled my clock radio out of the socket, attached it to an extension cord, and lugged it out to the driveway just in time to hear #40. I roller-skated in a circle, working on jumps and spins, as he counted them down. It didn't matter whether I liked the songs, and frankly, there is a limit to the excitement a child can work up over Air Supply. But who cares; the star of the show was Casey. He pronounced each artist's name, crisply and respectfully. He gave each band equal weight, even Franke and the Knockouts. Even Get Wet. He told us that this thing, pop music, was a thing to be taken seriously, no matter what the rest of the world told us. Casey got it.

By the time he got to #15, I'd have to shower and get ready for Mass, but once a song made it that far up the charts, I'd heard it enough. Plus, if Father Shea did a short enough homily, we'd make it back to the car in time to hear what was #1. A thrilling moment, even during the grim, endless reign of "Bette Davis Eyes."

My roller-skating got pretty good with all that practice every Sunday, so I took my act on the road. There was a roller rink a couple towns over, and it cost only a couple bucks to spend a weekend afternoon there. I couldn't get anyone to go with me, and I could not have cared less. Each week I wore the same thing: maroon rugby shirt with horizontal khaki and navy stripes, blue jeans held up by rainbow suspenders. I requested the same song: "I'm Alive" by ELO, from the *Xanadu* soundtrack, and I skated around and around on my own. Only when the DJ announced the snowball—where one couple skates, and then breaks up and finds new partners, and then two couples become four, and so on, until everyone who has experienced puberty has a skating partner—would I take a crucial break for Bugles and a Mr. PiBB. *I don't need to be in a couple,* I figured. *I've had my Xanadu moment and I'm dressed like Mork. To ask for more would be selfish.*

And then in a flash, my brothers were off to college. Dan went to Notre Dame, Steve two years later to Creighton. The timing could not have been better: Dan hit college just in time for the golden age of what we were then calling "college music." He came back home from his freshman year with a Peaches Records & Tapes crate full of new treasures: the Clash, Squeeze, the Specials and the Pretenders and the English Beat. He caught the wave at the perfect time, and I got to reap the benefits: while he was gone at his summer job selling shirts at Brooks Brothers downtown, I rifled through and listened to messages from another planet: Split Enz's *True*

Colours, XTC's *Black Sea,* U2's *Boy.* Fine bands whose best quality was that nobody else at school had ever heard of them.

Steve had hopped off the soul train by the time he got back from his freshman year; Magic 108 was starting to work some rap songs into their rotation. *Anyone can rap,* we thought. *That's not music.* We agreed it was a fad that wouldn't even make it to 1983. The only thing keeping him in the fold was a young artist out of Minneapolis named Prince, and his protégés The Time. Filthy dirty funk music. Exactly what the country's Catholic white boys didn't know they needed.

When they moved out, cable TV moved in. We didn't get it for a few years, despite my begging—"Filth! Vulgar! N.O. spells *NO,*" Mom said—but my friend Pete down the street did, and we organized a barter system: he could come to my house and play the video games his parents denied him, and I would be able to spend an equal amount of time sitting in front of MTV at his. I remember the first time we flicked over to that channel together and were greeted with the sexily menacing pleather-and-neon jungle of Total Coelo's "I Eat Cannibals." We sat back in slack-jawed satisfaction and didn't move for months.

What to the untrained eye looked like vegging out in front of the television was actually me silently plotting a way to crawl inside.

Looking back, I think my family raised me right. There were probably some lessons about decency and fairness and manners in there somewhere—who can remember?—but the main thing my parents and brothers taught me by example was how to appreciate pop culture and music. I want to thank them and also explain to them that I am their fault.

At the time of writing, both of my brothers listen to Toby Keith and my parents pretty much exclusively watch Fox News, at the volume level of a My Bloody Valentine concert. It's heartbreaking, but at least they left me something valuable before they checked out.

Seven Pieces of Pop Culture That Prevented Me from Leading a Normal Life

THE POP culture of the mid- to late 1970s had no interest in entertaining children, which worked out beautifully because I had no particular interest in being a child. I was a sponge for all the music, TV, and movies I could get my eyes and ears on, and even the silly shit left a mark forever. Here are a few of the reasons I can't hold down a regular job.

Grease, The Original Motion Picture Soundtrack

I begged for and received the soundtrack to *Grease* (a movie I had seen and not understood) in the summer of 1978 and swiftly went about the business of learning every single word, which required me to stop my father in the middle of his lawn mowing and ask, "What's a tit?" *Grease* was a pretty filthy soundtrack—much filthier than the presence of a pre-"Physical" Olivia Newton-John would suggest—and while it may have worried my parents to hear me singing "she's a real pussy-wagon" and "get your filthy paws off my silky drawers," what they really should have had them concerned was such early, prolonged exposure to Stockard Channing.

The Carol Burnett Show

If subtlety had been invented in the mid-1970s, it did not get through the doors of CBS Television City. Carol and the gang were turned all the way up all of the time, which for a child's first exposure to sketch comedy is actually perfect. They did show-length parodies of *Mildred Pierce* and *Gone With the Wind*—movies I had not seen—and yet I ate it up. Could Harvey Korman have pulled it together once in a while? Sure. But it was the first time I saw grown-ups goofing off in an effective, efficient way, and I wanted in. (Honorable mention goes to Cher. In the early '70s, we said to Cher, "Listen: we know that you have a lovely, husky singing voice and a body for Bob Mackie gowns, but can you also do broad comedy?" And she said: "You know what? Let's find out together.")

"Hot Stuff"—Donna Summer

Children don't really get euphemism—sexual euphemism, particularly. So when this song came out, and Donna Summer was on the radio pleading for some hot stuff baby this evening, I assumed she was asking for a soothing bowl of clam chowder. I thought: *Donna Summer is enthusiastic about a hearty soup, and she doesn't care who knows it.* As with most truths you learn in adulthood, this one really disappointed.

"Lay Down Sally"—Eric Clapton

What I loved about this one was the emotional bait and switch Eric plays with Sally. He spends most of the song begging her to stay the night, and then once he's convinced her, he's all: "Don't you ever *leave*?" Man, isn't that adulthood right there, I thought.

Just when you think you know where you stand with someone, they toss you right out on your ass. And then an older kid in the neighborhood set me straight. It's more like: "Don't you *ever* leave," like, "Keep staying here, the way I've been telling you to do," which is pretty straightforward, as love messages go. Basic.

"Same Old Lang Syne"—Dan Fogelberg

The first 45 I ever bought. It's about a guy who runs into his old lover in the frozen foods section, and they reminisce and lie about how happy they are over a six-pack of beer in the back-seat of her car. I want to say it's Christmas Eve, but maybe that's just my memory adding more drama. Then he gets out and she drives off into the night and the snow turns into rain and nobody gets what they want and now Dan Fogelberg is dead. I was nine. This song posited adulthood as a series of disappointments I couldn't wait to grow up and face.

"I've Never Been to Me"—Charlene

In which a dissolute woman bothers some lady on a bench and launches unbidden into the story of her life. She's seen it all: she's been to the Isle of Greece, she's sipped champagne on a yacht, she's done it with a priest—outside on someone's lawn, even. Charlene has been there and back. And in the middle of the song, she stops singing entirely and just starts talking to the poor lady, who by now I imagine has driven off, with Charlene following on foot: "You know what love is?" she asks, and we know she's going to tell her: "Love is that husband you fought with this morning, the same one you're going to make love with tonight," she says. Charlene is dropping some truth bombs, and, not knowing many Charlenes—or many grown-ups, for that matter—I assumed she was Charlene Tilton, famous at the time for her work as loose cannon Lucy Ewing on *Dallas* (and for being a giant coked-up mess in the front rows of music awards shows with her then-husband Johnny Lee). And then she gets back to singing, this time about the unborn children who might have made her complete, and my mother would tsk and say "Oh, for God's sake,"—*O, fer Gad's seek*—and change the channel because we are Catholic, and abortion in pop music is not going to fly. But such drama! If the people in my subdivision seemed to have it all together, Charlene was coming the fuck apart, and I wanted to listen again and again.

"Magic Man"—Heart

This song has it all: passion, poetry, that synth break in the middle that makes you feel like you're on a spaceship. Plus it came out right in that 1970s moment when cults were at their peak, so I could imagine that it was about some mysterious figure in a white robe who came into the Wilson sisters' lives and hypnotized them, permanently transforming them into pure beings of rock and roll by sheer force of will and charisma. That guy could be around any corner. He could mesmerize you, too.

Now of course I realize it's probably just about getting finger-blasted.

3

Let's Go Crazy

THIS IS ONE OF MY MOST VIVID MEMORIES FROM CHILD-hood: I'm in the backseat of the family station wagon. My father is driving, telling my mother about something that happened in the office that day. He's a gesticulator, my dad, and he's really going to town on this story. His face is serious as the tale unfolds—something about spreadsheets? Portfolios? I don't know—yet my mother's face beams. She is smiling like he is telling her she's just won a cash prize of a hundred thousand dollars.

"What?" my father asks her.

"What *what*?"

"Why are you smiling? This story isn't all that funny."

"No, I know. I just don't want them to think you're yelling at me." And she gestures around us at the other cars on Highway 40.

In Catholic St. Louis, it is customary to put on a show for the rest of the world. You need to tell everyone around you that you are normal, and that everything is just fine. It is vital to keep up appearances, even for strangers, who, like you, are traveling at seventy miles an hour on a major highway.

You don't want to stand out. You want to be just like everyone else, maybe just a little bit better.

You for sure do not want to be what I was starting to figure out I was.

Gayness was a thing that people recognized by the early 1980s, but if there were any actual gay people among us, they kept it to themselves. Homosexuality was no longer illegal and underground, but it wasn't cool yet; Neil Patrick Harris was a toddler. We were in between, where gay people were mostly just there to be the butt of a massive percentage of the jokes in movies and on television and in real life, and not only could you not point this out or act like it bothered you, you did your best to avoid the word "butt" altogether, because the way you said it might give you away.

"Gay" was the preferred put-down among boys at the time, as it had been for years and would continue to be for many more, and it was a bit of a catch-all. While on paper it was very simple—anything that is cool is *not gay,* everything else *is*—in practice it was extremely complicated. Here is an incomplete list of things you could do to get yourself called a faggot as an American thirteen-year-old boy in 1984:

Display enthusiasm
Wear your backpack over both shoulders
Walk faggy (precise definition is fluid)
Wear argyle socks
Use big words
Not care much for The A-Team
Say the answers to things in class
Have a female friend
Know the words to Matthew Wilder's "Break My Stride"
Smile

In this environment, if you do not fit into the narrow, ever-shifting definition of what is masculine and therefore acceptable, life becomes a constant, exhausting effort to stay on what you are told is the right side of the cool/gay divide. You study older, more secure-looking boys for cues on how to talk, how to walk, how to yawn and cough and laugh, so that you will be acceptable. You make a hundred thousand micro-decisions about your behavior before lunch. You never exactly get it—you can't wear coolness and masculinity as effortlessly as the boys who are born with it—but you can fool some people. And when you can't, when you hear things like "man up" or "quit being such a faggot," you don't recognize these comments as bullying, you take them as you would notes on a performance. *I should be better at not being me,* you think. *Thanks for the reminder.*

(What's especially odd is that in 1984 you could get called a faggot, and then the guy who said it to you would put his headphones back on and resume listening to Twisted Sister or Mötley Crüe or whatever other group of men in bustiers, fishnet stockings, and full faces of L'Oréal products he had been enjoying before he accused you of being gay for holding your books the wrong way.)

To be a young gay kid is to work around the clock. You start to feel feelings and you immediately get to work telling yourself that you're not feeling them, or that they're a phase, or that they're motivated by some part of you that's not the real you—a curiosity that's spun out of control, a sickness, a demon, if you're religiously inclined.

And the work never ends. The foreman never rings the dodo bird, you do not slide down the tail of the dinosaur, you never get to shout "Yabba-dabba-doo." You work and you never stop working and you never tell anyone, even yourself, that you're working.

You develop crushes, but you don't recognize them as crushes. You just find yourself drawn to that boy who talks and walks and yawns/coughs/laughs like he's never had to think about how to. You think about him all the time. You want to be him and you want to be with him, but you immediately tell yourself that you don't. You feel love and then you feel shame for feeling love. You pretend none of this is going on, because if anyone suspects that something is wrong, they might figure out exactly what is wrong, and then it's all over. So you push it down. You push it down and you smile, but not too much, because, again, smiling's pretty gay.

You put yourself through this process over and over, in the years when you are learning how to be a human being, and you get so good at it that it becomes involuntary. It's like a computer process, and like computers, you're getting faster and more efficient. You get so good and so quick that after a while you don't even notice yourself doing it.

+   +   +

The process really got moving for me in seventh grade, the year all the boys from my class got dropped into a new all-male Thunderdome of testosterone, an all-boys Catholic school called Priory that was run by Benedictine monks from England. Each form—grades seven through twelve were *forms one through six* there, because of the Britishness—contained fifty boys in jackets and ties and khakis, learning Latin by memorization. The "Total Eclipse of the Heart" video, without Bonnie Tyler as headmistress.

By form one, most of my male friends had magically trans-
formed into young men, seemingly all at once. They filled
out, grew taller, gained confidence. In our free periods, about
forty-five of the boys in form one would run outside to tackle
and throw balls at one another. The rest of us would do things
like talk at length about Bonnie Tyler's "Total Eclipse of the
Heart" video.

The clubhouse for those who preferred Culture Club to
contact sports was the Candy Store, the snack window over-
looking the Junior House field. We volunteered to work the
register because they had a boom box with a cassette player
in there, and for us, proximity to a cassette player was crucial.
Me, Ned, Derek, Tim, and Tom, and Phong No, the wildly
effeminate Korean American kid. We played Duran Duran.
We played Wham! We taped the Hot 9 at 9 off KHTR every
night, and then played it in the room and debated each song's
merits. (Stevie Wonder's success with "I Just Called to Say I
Love You" felt unearned; he was coasting.)

The roughhousers and horseplayers would come to our
window, hair slicked to foreheads with sweat, Tuffskins grass-
stained. They'd order their Andy Capp's Hot Fries and Vess
Whistle Orange Sodas and little tiny powdered doughnuts.
(Phong No would insist on proper nomenclature when orders
were placed. "Gimme the little tiny powdered doughnuts," a
kid would say. "The Donette Gems . . . ?" Phong corrected,
with just a trace of his mother's accent: *Donette-ah Gems-u?*
"Yeah," the kid would concede. "Gimme the Donette Gems.")
It was in this room that we witnessed the Thompson Twins'
commercial breakthrough ("Is he saying 'Hold my cold Italian heart' at the end there? Are they *Italian*?" Tim asked, and
we all agreed they look more British. Scottish, maybe). It was

here that we compared Swatches (while the all-black one was impossible to read, it was preferable to the white one with the polka-dots, which showed dirt almost immediately). It was here on Monday mornings that we would relive *Friday Night Videos*, which we all watched and recorded and studied like our Latin conjugations (what exactly was this underground lair to which Simon Le Bon descended in the "Union of the Snake" video? In "Dance Hall Days," were Wang Chung saying they were "cool on Christ"? How would one do the Neutron Dance? What did it all mean?).

Michael Jackson was everything back then, and the strangest thing about him was that his speaking voice seemed sort of high. To have had the pop perfection that was singles four through six of *Thriller*—to review: "Wanna Be Startin' Somethin'," "Human Nature," and "P.Y.T. (Pretty Young Thing)." Single number seven, "Thriller," uncoupled from its truly epic and groundbreaking video, is garbage and in your heart you know it—as the soundtrack of early puberty and entry into junior high is a privilege for which I am grateful every day of my life. I mean, some poor suckers get Alannah Myles.

We Candy Store Boys threw ourselves and our energy into pop culture, which, as luck would have it, was going through its most stealthily gay phase ever. Boy George performed in dresses and Annie Lennox in suits. George Michael urged us to wake him up before we went-went, and he did so in shorts that were very small, and when he promised us it would be warm in bed, his eyes rolled back in his head in sheer gay ecstasy. Nobody was out of the closet. The gay was all in the subtext, which most kids missed entirely, though in many cases we could go ahead and round it up to *text*. (I mean, "Relax don't do it when you wanna come"?) We unconsciously responded to it.

We also consciously responded to it. Over Donette Gems in the Candy Store the day after Madonna's "Material Girl" world-premiered on MTV, Derek and I relived every moment. I said, "He sends her these flowers, which she doesn't even want," and Derek said, "And then suddenly she's on this movie set."

"Right, with this gown."

"Yeah, and all these cute guys . . ."

Derek could stop time too.

". . . I mean *cool-looking guys* on either side of her, *anyway, it's a great video, right?*" and we just looked at each other for a long few seconds, him silently mortified, my eyes saying, "I've got you now, and if you cross me I will destroy you, and also which one's your favorite? Mine's the one two from her left."

We never talked about it again.

Phong No was the most effeminate kid of the bunch, and he didn't seem to care about it. He was obsessed with *Dynasty.* His *s*'s were so sibilant you could hear them two classrooms over. He wrote a song about fruit salad, to the tune of Bananarama's "Cruel Summer," that he would sing at lunchtime:

> *It's a fruit, fruit salad*
> *Nanners and waa-aa-termelons, a fruit*
> *Fruit salad*
> *It makes your mouth drool with saliva, it's true*
> *True! Fruit salad [etc.]*

Phong No either couldn't change his behavior or didn't feel a need to. Either way, in retrospect, Phong No is kind of my hero.

At the time, of course, outside of the Candy Store, we mostly pretended we didn't know him.

* * *

You can't stay inside the Candy Store forever. In the Catholic school tradition, we were also forced to be on sports teams at all times. When you're thirteen and the kind of person who'd rather talk about the quick evolution of Sheena Easton from Scottish pixie into some kind of angry sex worker, you kind of just go through the motions. You warm up and do drills with the team, and then when it is time for a scrimmage, you mostly sit on the bench. It's an unspoken arrangement you have with the coaches, and it's mutually beneficial; you would be a distraction on the field at best, an actual hazard at worst. So the gang from the Candy Store spent a lot of time on the perimeter of the playing field. We talked about whom we'd seen on the most recent *Solid Gold* ("I have the Nena album, if anyone wants to tape it," Derek told us). We discussed which track on Culture Club's *Colour by Numbers* was the best one (then as now, I rode hard for "Church of the Poison Mind"). We talked about how Pat Benatar had little individual secret goodbye handshakes for each of her fellow dime-a-dance girls in the "Love Is a Battlefield" video ("Those women have *seen* things," Tim said. "Those women have *lived*.")

In September and May, when the weather was warm, scrimmages would be shirts vs. skins, which would add at least two layers of emotional complexity to a situation that was already fraught. The rest of the year we'd wear red and blue fishnet tops over our sports clothes, which in the wake of Madonna's "Lucky Star" video were right on trend.

But there were some boys—most boys, really—who when it came time for practices and scrimmages instinctively knew what to do. They'd look down the field and calculate a clear route all the way to the end, like some kind of robot sports person, like the Terminator, and they'd run like hell, and they'd score however many points you get for getting there. And the other kids in jerseys of the same color would give them high-fives or chest-bumps or—I swear this is true—just pat them, without hang-ups or hesitation, right on the butt. And the owner of the butt that had been patted would just accept it. Like: my friend has patted my butt; this means I have done well. It was straight-up fascinating to me, and it is a thing that even now I cannot imagine myself doing, not even now that I can drink.

But here's the part that I truly couldn't and still can't quite believe: sometimes a boy would send the ball to the wrong person, or someone from the other team would knock him down, or he would break one of the five million rules about where your hands or feet are supposed to go, and his plan wouldn't work out at all. It might even result in the other team scoring. It might result in the other team *winning*. And if it did, this boy would get upset for a second or two, and then just shake it off. He wouldn't worry about what everyone else thought about him, or about how many rungs his mistake had knocked him down the social ladder, or about whether he actually did suck. He would just have made a mistake, as people do, and he and his friends would live to touch one another's butts another day. This was astonishing to me. This was like flight.

Jim was one of these boys. He came to Priory from a different grade school, so I met him at age twelve, fully formed. But, like, formed out of marble. He was self-assured, he was cool. He had what young and/or terrible people are now calling *swag*. He threw a spiral so perfect even I could notice it. In our first few football games against other boys' schools, he scored about 50 percent of the touchdowns and exactly 100 percent of the ones I noticed. He ascended quickly and decisively into student council. I was fascinated by him. I noticed what he wore and how he walked—and talked and laughed and coughed and yawned and *was*—and I tried to mimic it. He had jet-black hair and pool-water blue eyes, and dude could wear the hell out of a pair of Tuffskins. When we read Thomas Mann's *Death in Venice* in the winter trimester of form one, and Aschenbach described Tadzio as a Greek statue, I thought: *Oh, I feel you, Aschenbach.*

Everybody liked Jim. But I *really* liked Jim. And it thrilled and frightened and confused me at the same time. I felt constant, sexy panic.

When I started to have erections, and I started to, you know, *do something about them*, I would force myself to think about Teri Copley, the maid from NBC's Saturday night sitcom *We Got It Made*. She seemed correct to me: blond, busty, the mutually agreed-upon heterosexual male fantasy. And at the beginning, my desire to be normal would provide enough fuel. Really, pretty much anything will do for a boy in junior high. But then, oh, no, oh, God help me, one of those sophomore JV football players' calves would pop into my head, or the beefy forearm of a senior. No, Dave, no. This is about Teri. *Focus on Teri. That's right.* And then without my even hearing him come in, Corey Hart would show up out of nowhere and I'd realize I was in that jail cell from the "Sunglasses At Night" video. He would just rip off that white shirt and let me see the whole chest-hair situation the cover of *First Offense* hinted at. And then I'd come, and the joy would rush out of my body, and guilt and shame and nausea would rush in to fill the space, and I'd pray to God to just let me hold on to the Teri Copley fantasy through the whole process, just once.

(Teri's a born-again Christian preacher these days, incidentally. I take credit for making the introduction between her and God.)

If the boys of the Candy Store were going through the same struggle at the same time, which time has revealed that about half of us were—Ned spent a lot of time checking on the whereabouts of Brian, a form-two boy with a cool haircut; Derek always laughed a little too loudly at the young English teacher's jokes; Phong No was Phong No—we kept it to ourselves. We threw our energy into Tears for Fears. We had no choice.

My parents eventually relented and got us cable, and the importance of MTV in all this simply cannot be overstated. If you were a kid on the margins, you could turn on your television and get a window into a world you could see yourself in someday. It was reassuring, an "It Gets Better" video with a beat. I wanted to be like these strange people in Day-Glo clothing on my MTV. I longed to be free and sexual and unrepressed; you know, *British*. I requested a *Frankie Say Relax Don't Do It* T-shirt for Christmas, two sizes too large, as style dictated. I got it, and I wore it often, and I had no idea I was telling the world to hold off on ejaculating.

I also watched USA's "Night Flight" late on Fridays and Saturdays, when they were most likely to play the weird stuff. And I rode my bike into town each week to buy *Smash Hits* and *No.1*, the two glossy UK pop magazines the local newsstand imported. *Smash Hits* and *No.1* gave you bite-sized interviews with the likes of A-ha and Go West. They provided the lyrics for songs like King's "Love and Pride" and Paul Hardcastle's "19." They devoted their back pages to the charts, which were full of familiar hits by Madonna and Billy Ocean, but also mysterious UK up-and-comers like Steve Arrington and Hazell Dean. Every song and artist featured in these magazines instantly and automatically became one of my favorites, whether I was actually familiar with them or not.

(No, but really: *Smash Hits* hipped me to the existence of a UK Top 10 hit called "Starting Together" by a young Brit named Su Pollard, who got a two-page spread and a pull-quote: "I used to do tap dance shows for me mum, right there on the lino!" I never did hear her song, but her sassy specs, creative name spelling, and devil-may-care hair spikes convinced me she was the real deal. I wrote her name across the spine of my binder in bold letters: SU POLLARD. In the years since, I have done my research, and it turns out Su Pollard was the star of a family-hour sitcom called *Hi-de-Hi!* and a regular on the morning chat shows. What I did at age thirteen is the equivalent of a British kid today trying to earn credibility by scrawling KELLY RIPA across the cover of a notebook.)

I remember where I was the first time I heard Simple Minds' "Don't You Forget About Me." This is easy because I was where I always was from ages twelve to sixteen, which was in our family room, two inches in front of the television. But it quite simply knocked me dead. It had everything I wanted from a song and a video: a sweeping chorus. A Scot in a tweed suit. Scenes from *The Breakfast Club.* It was fresh, urgent, vital. I heard it the way I imagine the people of 1971 heard "What's Going On" for the first time, except the cause of our generation was getting teenagers to see the new Molly Ringwald movie. (We did see it opening weekend, by the way, us

Candy Store boys, despite it having been rated R. It was playing at the Crestwood Plaza two-screener, whose other theater was playing *Places in the Heart*. We convinced our parents and the box office of this cinema that we were spending a Saturday afternoon watching a Sally Field/Danny Glover 1920s farm drama, the way groups of adolescent boys are known to do.)

I had to have "Don't You Forget About Me." I had to get this song inside of me. I hopped on my bike and went to the Record Bar with my allowance in my pocket. It had just arrived, as had a brand-new single from a band so fresh they hadn't even been featured in *Smash Hits* or *No.1* yet: The Smiths' "How Soon Is Now?" I pulled it out and stared deeply into it. The guy at the counter saw a kindred soul, despite a grand whoosh of hair that blocked one eye. "Wanna hear it?"

I nodded yes. He grabbed it out of my hands, stuck a 45 adapter in its hole, popped it on the turntable, and introduced me to Morrissey. "I am the son and the heir of a shyness that is criminally vulgar."

I was hearing my story without even realizing it.

I bought it immediately, and a tiny Smiths button besides.

Biking home, I ran into Andy, a big, sporty kid from my class. "You went to Record Bar? Lemme see." I handed him my bag. "What are The Smiths?"

"They're a band. They're British."

"Ah." He nodded his approval.

"They're awesome."

He looked harder into the austere yellow cover and the blocky, utilitarian lettering. And then he looked at me. "This stuff looks weird." But it didn't sound like an insult. He said it with something like fear. Respect.

"Yeah. They are. They're *weird*."

I smiled, because I finally had a thing. I was *weird*. *We* were weird: me and the Candy Store Boys and Morrissey and Go West and Su Pollard. We were the future. We were not to be fucked with.

I also smiled because a bigger kid was going through my Record Bar shopping bag and I didn't want anyone driving past to think that I was being robbed or bullied.

4

The Edge of Heaven

WHEN YOU'RE IN THE MIDDLE OF YOUR TEENAGE years, all you want to do is be an adult. And in the middle of the 1980s, pop culture seemed to want that for you. Teenagers voluntarily listened to albums by middle-aged and/or bald guys like Phil Collins, Peter Gabriel, and Steve Winwood. The big show on ABC was *Moonlighting*, where Bruce Willis and Cybill Shepherd—both openly in their thirties—solved crimes and threatened to have sex with each other. In the monologue of the first episode of the 1986–1987 season of *Saturday Night Live*, host Sigourney Weaver brought out playwright Christopher Durang to give a quick, tongue-in-cheek dissertation on the work of German playwright Bertholdt Brecht. I will repeat: *there was a playwright on* Saturday Night Live *once*. These were heady times. It felt like American culture wanted me to be thirty-two with a loft in TriBeCa, to read all the books, to be glib. I was into it.

I was fifteen in 1986—too young for a proper job, too old to spend all day at the neighborhood pool, just the right age to start plotting an escape. Having left the Candy Store behind for the summer, Ned and I hatched a plan: there was a summer school for artsy kids in St. Louis called the Mark Twain Summer Institute, Mr. Twain being one of Missouri's prized offspring. You would select a course of study—creative writing, dance, drama, painting, or for some reason, economics—and spend six weeks of your summer working at it. It was all we wanted to do. (It was *almost* all we wanted to do; I had seen an ad for the Bennington July Program in the back of my parents' *New York Times Magazine*. A summer doing white drugs in Vermont with young Bret Easton Ellises would have been a non-starter.) I begged my parents to enroll me in the creative writing program for the summer. They did. So did Ned's. We couldn't wait.

We arrived dressed exactly as we would have been on a casual spring Friday at Priory—madras shorts, a sensible Polo—and immediately felt out of place. On the first day of Mark Twain, it was clear: the weird kids were in charge here. These were kids who took dance seriously, kids who had thought their haircuts all the way through. These were boys who could rock a Guess jean with confidence. These were wearers of black trench coats, even in the punishing Missouri humidity. There would be a new social order here.

The creative writing teacher was a professor at nearby Washington University with a pushbroom of a mustache, and the class was a cross-section of a city I'd only seen a sliver of. Black kids from up North. Old-money kids from the Central West End. A girl in a black silk cape and matching lipstick—Tabitha, with a long *i* and the accent on the second syllable. Surely she had been regular-style *Tab*itha when school had let out in May, but here she would be Ta*by*tha.

And then a boy flounced in, a few minutes late for the first session. A boy with blond ringlets over his right eye, wearing a black turtleneck sweater. A leather satchel—a purse?—hung off his shoulder. "Ugh," he said, sweeping his swoosh of hair off his forehead, "forgive me, I'm Frederick and I'm always late, I'm the *worst*." He threw himself into an empty chair. "What have I missed?"

Coming from an all-male high school where we expressed our masculinity by being terrified to stand out in any way, I had simply never seen a person like Frederick. He gesticulated wildly, turtleneck sleeves pulled far past his hands, like a hyperactive Muppet. He was proudly effeminate. He might as well have been from another planet. I was fascinated.

We spent the first class getting to know one another, talking about what we liked to read and what we hoped to write and who we were. Conversations like children imagine grown-ups having. Frederick liked *Less Than Zero*—"Well, who *doesn't*?" I said. I hadn't read it yet—and wanted to write something real, raw, poetic. I was into John Cheever and wanted to write short stories. "I like your hair, Fred," said one of the North County girls. "You look like that guy from Simply Red." And he did. "We'll call you Simply Fred," said another. He hid his face behind his turtleneck sleeves and laughed. "Oh, I hate it!" He loved it.

Our first assignment was to walk to the nearby St. Louis Art Museum and look around. Get inspired. Find something we like and stare at it until it begins to look unfamiliar. Just go interact with art and meet back by the front door in an hour. When we got back, we got a project: write a story about what we'd just seen. If it was a portrait, tell that person's life story. If it was a statue, make that person a character. If it was abstract, tell a story with the emotion that it made you feel. There were no wrong answers. I had literally never been told to do anything like this. I nearly cried, I was so happy.

Ned and I were in heaven at Mark Twain. We consoled the

drama kids through their weekly breakdowns. We read someone's older sister's issues of *Tatler*. We watched the dance class rehearse the piece they had choreographed about the Museum of Westward Expansion; these motherfuckers were *actually dancing about architecture!*

We watched one boy from the dance class in particular, every day. Thick like a football player, but graceful. Masculine, yet, you know, in a dance class rehearsing a piece about a Mondrian painting. An ass and a pair of shoulders that were as exquisite at anything I'd seen at the museum. David. (No, I mean his *actual name* was David. But his resemblance to the statue was also not a thing you would miss.)

Ned said: "Everyone here is beautiful."

I said: "I know."

"I mean, like, the women are amazing here. We should, like, let's rate the women here."

"They're all *so amazing*."

"But, like, on a secret scale. Like, just our thing. So nobody knows what we're talking about."

"Totally."

"Should it be, like, numbers? No, numbers are banal. How about, like, breads?"

"So . . . like, a scale of Wonder White to . . . rye? Something like that?"

"Right. Except Wonder's the bottom."

"I *love* Wonder Bread." Ned gave me a look. I made a mental note: expand bread horizons.

Ned made up his mind: "Let's go cheese. Let's do it on a cheese scale. Like, at the top is Gouda."

"Gouda."

"Yeah. Like, Ornella Muti from *Flash Gordon* is so *Gouda*."

"You think so?"

"Oh, absolutely. I find Italian women far more attractive than American women."

So we settled on cheese as the scale we would use to talk about women, and we did it on a scale of Gouda to Velveeta, which was a betrayal of my own personal taste, because I loved Velveeta, and also because we were using this scale to rate women, which neither of us actually liked. But we did it a lot: Susanna Hoffs was Gouda; the other Bangles were mostly Swiss. Sandra Bernhard was Stilton with Gouda potential. The drama teacher was gouda for an older woman—*aged* Gouda.

I began reading *Less Than Zero* immediately. It is a depressing read, full of drugs and rape and decadence, but it was very Gouda, because of this: There is a part in the book where the protagonist, Clay, wakes up in bed with a male friend and then gets up and casually gathers his clothes from the boy's living room while the housekeeper tidies up. That's the whole thing: it is suggested that our main character has had some kind of sexual encounter with another male, but it is only that—a suggestion. I reread that passage roughly four thousand times. It was easily accessible gay porn.

After classes, we'd go to the nearby art-house cinema and watch movies they didn't play in the suburbs. *Something Wild. After Hours. Mondo New York.* Laurie Anderson's *Home of the Brave.* We'd smoke cigarettes from the tobacconist next door. Dunhills, please; we'd pretended to outgrow Marlboro Lights within the first week.

These were kids with whom I could trade mixtapes. I'd throw on some Replacements ("Left of the Dial" having the perfect mix of joy and pathos), some Marshall Crenshaw (there is a wealth of goodness beyond "Someday, Someway"; besides

Tommy Keene, the man is America's greatest unsung hero),
and some vintage Monkees (whose sitcom was being rerun on
MTV that summer). At the time, I was well aware of IRS Records and their hip roster of artists: The Go-Go's, The Police,
REM. An IRS logo on an album cover—a black-and-white
drawing of a G-man in Wayfarer sunglasses—was a mark of
quality. A *Good Housekeeping* Seal of Approval for kids who
based their identities on which bands they listened to. But the
Mark Twain kids dug deeper. They were into acts on *Enigma
Records:* Don Dixon, Game Theory, Rain Parade. I had been
trumped. Frederick made me and Ned and Ta*by*tha mixes of
Cocteau Twins, The Fall, "You're Never Fully Dressed Without a Smile" from *Annie. Oh, shit, Simply Fred,* I thought. *You
are good at this.*

I spent the six weeks writing stream-of-consciousness poetry, overwrought one-act plays, short stories about life on the
streets of the big city (by a boy from a nice house in the suburbs). My characters swore a lot, because they could, because I
could make them. I tried to write strange things, because I was
in a place where nobody would make me feel strange about it.

That year, my family had moved into a bigger house with
a huge backyard and a tennis court we would never use, and
I decided I should throw the Mark Twain goodbye party. My
parents chaperoned from inside, over a rented movie, while
outside, artsy fifteen-year-olds threw down. Kids furtively
smoked weed out of Diet Slice cans. Dancers did some free-
form work to Scritti Politti album tracks on the smooth surface
of the tennis court. The scent of cloves hung in the air. I was
living the less-rapey parts of *Less Than Zero.*

David came to the party, and he smoked, and he swayed to
The Cure. Ned and I kept our eyes on him and talked too ex-

citedly about all the women at the party who were Gouda. We sneaked drags off cigarettes and drank plastic tumblers full of Matilda Bay wine cooler from a box someone brought and hid in the bushes. And then David's ride showed up, and he had to go, and he hugged us both on the way out. My heart soared and apparently so did Ned's, because I don't remember if he said it first or I did, or if we said it together, but somebody said: *"David is Gouda."* And we looked at each other and walked over to an area of the tennis court where nobody was, where we talked about where literally every other boy we knew fell on the cheese scale.

Simply Fred was at the party, too, and we could have waved him over into the conversation, but we didn't. We didn't say this out loud, but looking back, I think the reasoning went something like: *He is gay. We are just boys who have intense sexual attraction to other boys. Whole different thing.*

We continued that way for the rest of our high school career. We'd socialize, and then one of us would give the signal, and we'd escape to a corner or one of our cars to talk about which boys we were attracted to. Later, we'd share which ones we thought we liked, and later still, which ones we thought we *loved*. Throughout the rest of high school, the most we were able to admit to ourselves was that we were bisexual, despite the fact that neither of us said even one thing about even one girl, even one time.

After the summer ended, the Mark Twain kids and I would talk on the phone once in a while. They were back to their underfunded public schools or art magnet programs; I was back among the coats and ties. But we were new people. We'd found the confidence that comes with finding your tribe. We'd send letters to one another—diary entries, really—with song and book recommendations. How had I never bought Kate Bush's *Hounds of Love?* How had Simply Fred not tried that first Crowded House record?

That autumn, my attention returned to Jim, who became the first kid in our class to get his license. For his sixteenth birthday, his parents leased him a brand-new Oldsmobile Cutlass Supreme, and our young adulthood officially began. And the first Friday of his life as a driver, Jim stopped by my locker.

"Holmes."

"Yeah?"

"What are you doing tonight?"

"I don't think I'm doing anything."

"A few of us are gonna drive around. You wanna come?"

I felt like a sweepstakes winner. *Me?* "Um, yeah! Sure." And he came and picked me up, and there were a few guys from our class in the car, and we just drove, because that was enough. I did an impression of the way the new French teacher said *"l'ouiseau,"* and my audience laughed. Even Jim laughed. I had a purpose and a new life, and Jim was my friend. I felt like that hotel maid in Joe Jackson's "Steppin' Out" video when she tries that dress on, just twirling and twirling and imagining her new life, but also tried on the spot to think of a more masculine thing to feel like.

In the winter of that year, Priory took a field trip to the local repertory theater to see *Steel Magnolias.* (I suppose we had to be exposed to women somehow.) It was one of those matinees where the entire audience is high school kids, which must be brutal on the performers. The parking lot was bright yellow with buses, and the theater was roaring with shouts and giggles.

And a few moments before the show began, I heard someone calling my name. Shrieking it, really. "DAAAAAAVE!"

It was Simply Fred. His sophomore class was here, too. He waved, a few inches of black fabric flapping past his hands, like an inflatable man outside a car dealership. "HIIIII!"

Everyone looked at him. And then everyone looked at me. *Everyone.*

"Hi, Simp . . . Hi, Fred—" I felt my face heat up. ". . . erick."

It may have been fine for him to go back to school and be who he'd been that summer, but the same wasn't true for me.

We looked at each other for what felt like a minute.

"Well, it's good to see you."

"Yeah!" I said. "Yeah, you too."

Me telling him "Not here," him telling me "I'm sorry," neither of us saying words.

He walked away. Slower this time.

I don't remember who said, "Is that your boyfriend, Holmes?" first, but within seconds it was nearly everyone, and I was spared only by the dimming of the lights.

I was in danger.

And then the curtain went up and we watched a play about a bunch of sassy women in a southern hair salon.

On the line to get back onto the bus, Ned pulled me aside. "Thank God he didn't see me. Are you okay?" I wasn't sure whether I was.

American pop culture wanted me to be a grown man. I was still a little boy.

Seven Fun Activities for When Your Straight Crush Becomes Your Friend

SO LET'S say the kid in your class who you idolize suddenly becomes one of your friends. It doesn't have to be weird and painful, it can be weird and painful and *fun*! Spend your entire high school career doing some or all of these:

Be With Him All The Time

If he talks to other people, he might find that he likes them. He might even like them better! This is simply too big a risk. In between classes, at lunch, after school, be there. Be the guy he talks to. Be the *only* guy he talks to.

Find Some Songs That Remind You of Him, Put Them All on a Mixtape, Listen to It All the Time

Bryan Ferry's "Slave to Love." The majestic ache of Heart's "Alone." Belinda Carlisle's robotic vibrato in "I Get Weak." Alison Moyet's "Weak in the Presence of Beauty," which is pretty much the same song. Put them all together—any many, many more!—on a Maxell ninety-minute tape and always have it on. Expert level: don't be aware that this mixtape is actually about him, just tell yourself that these are your favorite songs all of a sudden.

Call Him Your Best Friend, Immediately

People love this, teenage boys especially. It's just a fact: when you meet someone and you enjoy spending time with them, label it as quickly as you can. Everybody feels more secure that way. Do it!

Had a Fun Night Out? Go Tell Him About It

Everyone is starting to get their driver's licenses, and you and the other Candy Store Boys are starting to get invited to girls' school dances, because girls love boys who aren't afraid to be the first one on the dance floor and won't ever be sexually aggressive with them. Your social life is opening up. He'll want to know! When the dance and the after party are over, go throw pebbles at your very best friend's window, get him out of bed, and tell him everything that happened over late-night Fruity Pebbles and *Night Tracks*. Who needs sleep? Not him, probably!

Learn Some Fun Facts, Say Some Fun Facts

Your best friend might not be much of a talker. He might be the strong, silent type—a beguiling, mysterious, confident fellow who doesn't need to be making a sound at all times to prove his worth. Fuck that! He probably just doesn't know what to say. Casey Kasem can be a big help here; you can spit back some of his most useful facts: "Terence Trent D'Arby was born Terence Trent Howard in New York City!" "You know, Roxette is a duo now, but just a couple of years ago, they were successful solo artists in their native Sweden." "Huey Lewis calls his new album *Small World* a real departure!" Just fill the air with noise. Fill it!

When You Go to Pick Him Up for a Night Out, Wait a Few Minutes Before You Knock

Say his parents go to bed early so you can't ring the doorbell. Say he tells you to rap at the TV room window when you come to pick him up. Imagine the TV room is situated in such a way that the couch faces the window and when you go to knock on it, he's facing you. His perfect legs are up on the coffee table, his blue eyes are on the TV, but they're close enough to where you're standing that you can imagine he's looking *at you.* You can let yourself feel how it might feel to be this close to him, just a few feet away, the two of you staring at one another, feeling the same way, thinking the same thing. All around you, there's a whole world of social activities, but this is where you truly need to be. Right here, imagining. Do this for as long as you feel like. This behavior falls under the umbrella of activities we will come to refer to as "stalking," but that's not important right now. Stay. Take it in.

If Possible, Do All of This in the 1980s

Everything that is painful about homosexuality still being the love that dare not speak its name can actually work in your favor here. What in the twenty-first century would immediately be recognizable as a young gay boy with a massive, awkward crush on a beautiful straight boy can now just look vaguely inappropriate in ways nobody can quite articulate. You don't even need to tell yourself what you're doing or why you're doing it. Just do it.

I mean, it's not like you have a choice.

5

Drifting, Falling

I SPENT THE REST OF HIGH SCHOOL OBSESSING OVER music and Jim, trying desperately to appear like a normal boy. When it came time to start thinking about colleges, there was a part of me that wanted to go somewhere artsy, where I could wipe the slate clean, finally integrate all the disparate parts of myself, and prepare for adulthood—the way the rest of the Candy Store Boys were planning to.

Here's what I did instead, in mixtape and memory-fragment form, because it's too pathetic any other way.

1. "Achin' to Be"—The Replacements

I had originally had my heart set on Boston College, based on its name alone. It was college, it was in Boston, that was pretty much all I needed to know. Plus it was close enough to Colgate, where Jim would be. (The East Coast was all one ten-square-mile mystery to me. I hadn't gotten out of St. Louis much.) I had visions of ivy-covered buildings and touch football games on grassy quads. I had no idea what to study, but I knew it was time for me to grow up and get practical, which I did by making my top college choice based on theoretical plant life and imaginary roughhousing. I visited BC and it seemed fine, and then my father suggested we make the forty-five-minute drive to Worcester to visit Holy Cross, a place a few kids from Priory had gone in the past.

It was love at first sight. The campus was gorgeous. Dramatic. Set up from Worcester on a massive hill, all stately buildings and spires and columns. And as we took the campus tour, the students simply beamed. They shouted hello to one another. They were freshly scrubbed and glowed with love for themselves, one another, and, we have to assume, God. I immediately developed a crush on this place and everyone in it. I thought about autumn mornings and tailgate parties and visiting someone's parents' house on the Cape. It was a superficial connection we had developed, this place and I, but it felt real. What I was feeling, I now recognize, was the desire to *be* one of these people. To be proud and to beam and to look good. To have no issues with my identity. To put my love of popular culture in its proper place, behind more practical matters. To be a good Catholic and a grown man. *Holy Cross is the place for me*, I decided.

2. "Sowing the Seeds of Love"—Tears for Fears

Boston College accepted me, Holy Cross put me on the wait list, and because the object of my affection indicated that it didn't feel the same way, I suddenly became obsessed with making it want me. I wrote letters and asked the monks who liked me to do the same, and in August, HC relented and accepted me and I was all about it. (Michael Damien's cover of David Essex's "Rock On" made it to number one in July, so, really, all of America was making questionable decisions in the summer of 1989.)

As my parents and I pulled up at my dormitory and the station wagon was unloaded by a squadron of chipper sophomores in matching T-shirts, the new Tears for Fears boomed out of a fourth-floor room. It was the first time I'd heard it, and it was sweeping and majestic and matched my feelings. I was starting over. We all were. We were all hitting the reset button. We were going to find out who we were, together. From scratch. I'd never be on the outside again.

And then I went to my room and met my two roommates Brian and Mike, lifelong best friends from the same hometown just outside of Boston.

3. "What I Am"—Edie Brickell & New Bohemians

Our first event was a tailgate and barbecue down by the football stadium, and we mingled. I learned quickly that Holy Cross draws almost exclusively from New England, and New England is a big small town. Everyone seemed to know one another, or know someone from one another's hometowns. At the very least, everyone spoke the same language, which is the language of abuse. Mockery, I learned after many confusing and unpleasant months, is how people from New England show affection. It's how they show they like you, which is very confusing, because it's also how they show they don't like you, and they're just never going to tell you which it is.

A local cover band played the hits of the day, and the one sort-of hippie girl in our class danced blissfully. She had brown curls down to her breasts and looked a little like Edie Brickell, and she twirled and she smiled and her paisley skirt caught the sunlight. She was happy.

I watched. A group of kids from my hall walked up, watched

me watch her, and then watched her. Rich, an ROTC guy, spoke up: "What is she, *retahded?*" And everyone laughed. Twirling, even from a hippie girl, was a thing that would not be tolerated here.

4. "One Wind Blows"—Toad the Wet Sprocket

Situated as it was on the side of a massive hill, the campus received two radio stations, the college radio station WCHC and Worcester's hair metal station WAAF, and 90 percent of the students opted for the latter. The two most significant bands in my life as a freshman became Toad the Wet Sprocket and Warrant.

The campus was full of the kind of people I wanted to be and devoid of the kind of people I was, and if anyone else felt the same way, they were hiding it better than I knew how to. This was the kind of place where people got dressed up to go to class, and then went home, showered, and changed into a nice clean outfit for dinner and study. Everyone was putting his or her best foot forward, and I had forgotten how to walk.

It was this kind of place: once a month, someone would run out from the student center, where our PO boxes were, and shout "It's here! It's *heeeeere!*" And people would sprint inside to get the hot item of the day: the new J.Crew catalog. The students were generous and thoughtful: if someone knew their roommate would already have brought one home, they'd leave theirs out on a table near the mailboxes for someone less fortunate. Everyone would make their selections, and eight to ten business days later, everyone would model their new barn jackets or wide-wale corduroys.

5. "Cuts You Up"—Peter Murphy

Holy Cross was homogeneous to the extreme, and everyone seemed to know the rules of survival except me. I got a weekly DJ shift at the campus radio station WCHC and I was there all the time. Music was my drug and I needed relief, so I was always using. I worried I had made the wrong choice, and I didn't know how to go about fixing it.

Freshman year, our social options were limited unless we had fake IDs, and mine was questionable: I was David Knight from Simsquix, Montana, standing in front of what is clearly a posterboard backdrop in the rough shape of a Montana driver's license. It only worked in the most rugged of townie bars that were the most desperate for business. You didn't want to go there unless you were in a pack, and you couldn't assemble a pack because most people didn't have fake IDs. So unless there was an off-campus party and the news trickled down to us, we were stuck watching Blockbuster rentals in our rooms. When we finished our movies, we rewound (because we were kind) and we left them by our front doors, just in case anyone else wanted to watch them during the three-night rental period. The first time I did this, the guys across the hall grabbed my movie, and then two hours later there was a knock on my door. I answered, and they were all there, wearing faces of agitation. "What is *wrong* with you, Holmes?"

"Excuse me?"

"That is the weirdest movie we have ever seen." They handed it back to me and left, and I looked down at it. It was John Waters's *Hairspray*.

I was on a campus full of eighteen- to twenty-two-year-olds

who had never seen—and never would—a weirder movie than *Hairspray*. *Oh, dear God*, I thought, *what have I done?*

6. "You Happy Puppet"—10,000 Maniacs

I was afraid and lonely and I was tired of being afraid and lonely, and I needed a plan, because I couldn't spend every waking moment at the campus radio station numbing out to music. So I made a decision. I decided to *be* one of these people. I pasted a smile on my face and I joked around with people; I was always on. And then I decided I was not only going to be one of these people, I was going to be *the best one of these people*. Light on my feet. Quick with a quip. At every party, at every event, in every bar. I went through a disposable camera a week, making people take photos of me with all my new friends as proof. *Look, I belong here! Look at my friends! Wheee!* I was the last to leave every party because I was afraid that if I left anyone behind, they'd talk to each other and piece me together.

7. "Vogue"—Madonna

I had an impression of an effeminate gay man that I did a lot. A *lot*. Generally, when people do impressions of gay men, which in the twentieth century was a popular thing to do, they give their character a lisp: "Oh, Thergio, thtop it!" they'll thay. This is simply incorrect, from a linguistic anthropological standpoint. The gay accent—the sound some men make with their voices that marks them as homosexual whether they actually are or not—has no lisp. What it has is a hissing sibilance in the *s*. A sharpness. It is unmistakable, and it is not a speech impediment, and every gay man I have ever met who does not naturally use it in his speech does a spot-on impression of someone who does. It's necessary for survival in the years before you come out. To do a flawless stereotypical-gay-man impression is to distance yourself from stereotypical gay men, which for all you know means "all gay men." It is to say: you may suspect me of being homosexual, but here, let me take care of that. Let me do an impression of how ridiculous a real gay man sounds, and then go back to my serious, respectable normal voice, thereby giving you a comparison that proves conclusively that I am not *that*. You see the difference?

It is a thing we have all done, but it doesn't make it any nicer to look back on.

8. "Slack Motherfucker"—Superchunk

Being everywhere and everything to everyone took energy, which I replenished by sleeping all day, every day. I never went to class. I skipped lectures, I didn't read books, and I had no idea what my professors looked like. It was a clear cry for help, but you weren't supposed to need this kind of help by the time you got to college, so nobody answered. I took a logic class, and I never went, and because I never went, I failed it, and I failed even to see the perfect logic in that.

9. "Between Something and Nothing"—The Ocean Blue

These were my two speeds: socializing and sleeping. Either I was manically trying to dazzle or I was unconscious. When I was awake, I was trying on the trappings of adulthood, of maturity, or what I perceived them to be—the conversation, the clothing—but I was doing nothing academically because I had no idea what to do. I changed majors three times: pre-med, pre-law, English. Nothing took. I was sinking in quicksand.

10. "Fun and Games"—The Connells

By the end of my freshman year, I met a couple of people in my Acting 101 class, and they invited me to hang out on their hall across campus in Wheeler. These guys were more relaxed, more accepting, and I felt like I could breathe around them a little bit. Finally, I began to feel like I was finding my footing. But the die was cast: I'd let things go for too long to catch up academically. The Wheeler guys invited me to share their house when the whole campus went to Hyannis the week after spring finals, and I went. It was lovely, and they were lovely, and I was beginning to think that I belonged just as I was beginning to realize that I wouldn't be allowed to come back.

10. "Here's Where the Story Ends"—The Sundays

Back in St. Louis in May of 1990, I went to check the mail and there was a notice for a piece of certified mail from the 01610 area code. I knew in my heart what was in that envelope and all of the blood ran out of my head and into my stomach. I'd been kicked out. I could apply to come back after one year. My parents were furious and I was mortified, and we were all ignoring the clear message the universe was sending us.

11. "See a Little Light"—Bob Mould

In the 1990–91 school year, I lived at home with my parents and took night classes at Washington University in St. Louis. I was in with the retirees and the extension students, and I put my nose to the grindstone because I was determined to get back to Holy Cross and finish what I had started. I did my studying in the Wash U library, made a few friends just from striking up conversations there, and I started getting invited to fraternity parties. I went, because I had nothing else to do, and it wasn't until I got a couple of bids that I realized that what I'd been doing was "rushing." Nobody knew I was a night student, or if they did know they didn't care. I pledged Kappa Sigma. I went through ritual and became an active brother, and they asked me to direct the spring musical they did each year with the Kappa Kappa Gamma sorority—so it was clear they not only knew who they were dealing with, but wanted me around anyway. At the end of the year, I had a fraternity house to live in if I wanted to, and my grades were good enough that I could fully matriculate to the regular, daytime Washington University. Things were going well for me in St. Louis. I was succeeding, and I was succeeding as myself.

But I was determined to win back the favor of the one who had rejected me, so I reapplied after that year to Holy Cross and they let me back in and I went.

12. "Where'd You Go?"—The Mighty Mighty Bosstones

By the time I got back to Holy Cross, a whole year had happened without me there, and while I still had friends, it was hard to get back in step. Plus we were juniors now—or *they* were, I had to repeat sophomore year—so most of my friends had gone abroad. I was alone again, naturally.

13. "Silent All These Years"—Tori Amos

I was probably supposed to be going to a school where people had open meltdowns, and went through bisexual phases, and broke their legs jumping out of trees while on mushrooms, but I was determined to make my relationship with this very normal, very practical place work this time. As a compromise, I turned off everything that was unique about myself. I was still manically social, but I wasn't dealing with what was happening in my mind or soul or crotch.

14. "Kiss Them for Me"—Siouxsie and the Banshees

I made a lot of desperate, late-night phone calls to Ned all through college, just to hear the voice of someone who knew me. He went to Rice in Houston, a university for brainy kids, where he studied architecture with a side order of Foucault and Derrida and queer theory. "Queer theory?" I asked him. "What's that?"

"It's like poststructuralism? It's, like . . . we do, like, textual analysis? But from like a gay angle? It's like . . . I just wrote a paper about the butch/femme dynamic in *Laverne & Shirley*."

He was also out of the closet and part of an active and vibrant gay community on campus, dating up a storm. There were places where you could not only be out of the closet and be taken seriously, but also watch sitcoms for course credit. I had not *missed the boat* so much as *failed to understand the concept of boats.*

15. "Regret"—New Order

College was, all the way around, a weird and isolating experience, and I made it that way all by myself, so much so that even now I can't engage with it without using a whimsical framing device like this. I took the time in my life when I was supposed to be figuring out who I was, and I spent it trying to be a fictional character. Ultimately, I look on this whole time in my life the way you do when you're looking at a picture of yourself wearing some embarrassing and ill-fitting thing that you wore because everyone else was.

6

Everybody Loves Me but You

I N 1991, I WAS BACK AT HOLY CROSS, GRATEFUL FOR THE second chance it had given me, yet also suffering from a debilitating cocktail of sexual frustration and loneliness that I can only call *hornliness*. The campus's situation on the side of a massive hill in central Massachusetts forced everyone walking class-to-class and party-to-party to tackle inclines and stairs, which meant that there were alarmingly shapely thighs and calves as far as the eye could see, but none for me to touch. There was literally not one other openly gay student or faculty member. It was like being starving and penniless outside a Krispy Kreme that's just lit its hot doughnuts now sign. Excruciating.

Luckily for me, there was some rock-solid yearning music in 1991. The bands coming out of Boston sounded the way a sweater feels. They were autumn in aural form. I had The Lemonheads, The Blake Babies, Juliana Hatfield, and Buffalo Tom on a constant loop in my head and my Volkswagen Jetta.

On the other hand, there was also an entire Suzanne Vega album called *99.9F°* that was largely a concept album about AIDS, and I had a scorching case of HIV-infection paranoia. I'd occasionally been brave enough to drive myself down to Boston and explore the gay bars, where I met a handful of guys from other, more diverse schools. I hooked up with a couple of them over the course of a few months—just innocent, over-the-jeans kind of stuff—but I was so skittish and so poorly informed that I became convinced I was HIV-positive, and the fear drowned out the thrill. There was nowhere on campus to get tested because Holy Cross was a Catholic school, and I couldn't even conceive of the level of panic I'd face waiting to get a result at the free clinic, and then what if someone drove past the free clinic while I walked in? Then they'd know, then *everyone* would know. Staying terrified at all times and pretending everything was great felt like the wiser option. My full AIDS action plan was to steer clear of that Suzanne Vega album.

I wanted to be out of the closet for one reason and one reason only: to find a boyfriend. I wanted to send up a flare, a signal that said "I'm here and I'm gay and everything's fine," and if anyone saw it and came to find me, the fact that everything was not at all fine wouldn't even matter anymore, because we'd have each other.

I was too afraid to do it. But I had to do something.

The only thing I could think of was to write an anonymous letter to the school newspaper, *The Crusader*. I could tell my story. I could reveal that I was here, an actual homosexual, walking among the rest of the student body. And I could withhold my actual name. And then I could listen closely for everyone's reactions. I could force a conversation.

So I wrote the letter.

I agonized over the wording. I was determined not to sound sad or terrified, although I was. I avoided anything that might make it sound like I had anything approaching sexual feelings, as though I were not an anthropomorphic cartoon boner at every minute of every day. I was very careful not to sound like a human being with needs; it was too risky. I dropped the letter into the campus mailbox and I waited.

And they published it, word for word. It was right there when the paper came out Friday morning, dead center in the op-ed section. I have typed it out and included it here in full, and it is all I can do not to type in little interjections from the present day. Things like "I KNOW," and "SOMEONE PLEASE HELP THIS BOY," and "SOMEONE PLEASE SLAP THIS BOY."

> *To the editor:*
>
> *This may very well be the first letter this publication has ever received which has been inspired by a correction. Recently, a correction ran which stated that the recent forum on Gay and Lesbian rights was not the first time homosexuality was addressed on campus, that indeed two years ago a forum on sexuality was held, and that homosexuality was discussed there. The more I thought about that fact, the more absurd it seemed. Homosexuality has been discussed openly twice in 148 years at this school. There's something wrong with that. I love Holy Cross, normally I would be the last to criticize it. However, speaking as a homosexual man, I feel that something needs to be done about this.*
>
> *As I stated, I am a homosexual. And despite what some of you might think, I'm not alone here. Statistically speaking, ten to fifteen percent of the United States population is gay. That means there are anywhere between 260–390 gays and lesbians on this campus. We're everywhere, and we don't fit the stereotype. Speaking of*

myself, I don't lisp, can't decorate a room to save my life, and have never, ever vogued.

I have even been on a sports team and dated women. Like most of the gays and lesbians on campus, I'm your typical Holy Cross student. Look around you next time you go to Stoney's or Joe De's. Chances are at least one of the people you came in with is gay. We're your friends, your roommates, your teammates. And, be assured, we're not going to hurt you. Nothing could be further from my mind than being anything other than friends with the men I hang around with, and I know that the rest of us on campus feel the same way. Please don't feel threatened.

The reason why this is all so important to me right now is that I'm currently in the process of "coming out of the closet" and I have a few words of advice for anyone who's reading this. First for all you straight people out there: as I said before, you have a gay friend. And chances are you don't know it yet. The reason why you don't is because your friend is scared to death to tell you. You may be the most understanding person in the world, but the fact is that we live in a homophobic society. Gays are discriminated against on a regular basis, and are almost always referred to as something less than respectable.

It's downright terrifying for someone to tell his/her friends that he/she is part of this socially unacceptable part of the populace.

However, I do have faith in the students here. I think we're all enlightened enough to overcome our preconceived ideas and accept things which are foreign to us. And if any of you out there aren't, then you have the problem.

You can change your mind, we can't change our sexuality. Homosexuality isn't a sin, a crime, a disease or even (in the broader scheme of things) a problem. Homophobia is. But it's easily overcome. You owe it to your friends and to yourself to take the steps toward broadening your mind. And should your gay friend ever "come out" to you, please remember a few things. First: he/she is the same person he/she was before you knew about it. He/she is not suddenly your enemy. Second, it takes a lot of courage for someone to "come out," even more when one is "coming out" to a close friend, since they risk losing that friendship which they treasure. Recognize that. You may be completely repulsed by the idea of homosexuality, but that doesn't mean you need to be repulsed by your friend.

For those of you out there who are gay, I ask only this: don't be afraid to tell your friends. I know what it's like in the closet, since for all intents and purposes I'm still there. It's no fun. Yes, it's difficult to tell people, but it's worth it. You owe it to your friends and ultimately to yourself to be honest. I'm still not ready to let the world know, but after having told a few of my close friends here, I can honestly say I don't regret it. I remember vividly the first time I told someone here. I hemmed and hawed and talked circles around it for hours, then finally just came right out and said that I'm gay. I was scared to death to look my friend in the eye, I was prepared for him to get up and leave. But he didn't. He nodded and said "Okay," and smiled, and that was that. We talked about it, we even laughed about it, and at the end of the night, he thanked me for being honest with him. I can definitely say it was the best feeling I'd ever had. And the next day, we could still talk about it. We still do. No, he's not gay, and no, I had no ulterior motives in telling him. The only thing that's changed between the two of us is that our friendship has grown that much stronger. I'm not saying it's always going to be that easy for you, but it will always be that gratifying.

You'd be surprised how open-minded your friends can be, and you won't believe how great it feels to have that weight off your shoulders. This may be hard to accept, but you'll never be "straight." You can, however, be straight with your friends about your sexuality, and that's about the most admirable thing I can think of.

I didn't set out to change the world with this letter but I hope I've changed some people's outlook on things a little bit. Homosexuality will always be an issue. Just because Holy Cross is so conservative doesn't mean it should be swept under the rug here. I hope I've created something that will be debated among friends, something that can be talked about honestly and unapologetically. I sincerely hope that in the future, when the subject of homosexuality is discussed, all people here can take the steps either to come out of the closet, or to make it easier for others to do so. Maybe then, we can all talk about it the way we talk about other issues. Let's hope it's more than twice in the next 148 years.

Gay at the Cross

Please know that I am now, having typed that out in 2016, in a full-body cringe. But in 1991, I read it proudly, as though some smarter person had written it. I went over it again and again. I had done it. I was ready to see how the rest of the world would respond.

People responded in one of two ways:

1. They read it and paid attention to how closely and eagerly I listened when I asked their feelings about it. Eventually, they put two and two together like the international bright young things they were, said they were proud of whoever wrote it, and then had the grace to act surprised when I told them it was me. Or:

2. They read it, and assumed it had been written in jest. There were more than a few of these, and it stopped me dead every time. I had prepared myself for every possible outcome except this one. There were people in 1991, in a school of 2600 people, who could not believe there would be *one* homosexual among them. It knocked me off my feet, like Charlie Brown getting flattened on the pitcher's mound in a *Peanuts* cartoon.

But category two was a fraction of the size of category one, and I began to tell a few friends, and then they told a few friends, because that's the way a small college works, and then suddenly I was out. People knew. It was a *thing*. Someone would come up to me in a bar and say: "Dave, I think my little brother is gay; what should I do to make him feel comfortable enough to tell me?" And I would answer: "What is your name?" Being out ended up being a nonissue. We were learning to be good little Catholics at Holy Cross, acknowledging but never really talking about the hard stuff.

The letter got the Chaplain's Office talking. Holy Cross is

run by the Jesuits, a progressive order of priests (as orders of priests go), and it turned out they were waiting for someone to bring the issue to their doorstep. What they decided to do was issue a poll, through students' PO boxes, about sexual issues. Are you sexually active? Do you use contraception? How would you describe your sexuality: homosexual, heterosexual, or bisexual? The poll was a little intrusive and clumsy, but what are you going to do with celibates? I filled mine out, folded it up, sent it back through the mail, and began actively counting the minutes until the results would be published.

I went to a meeting of the Campus Activities Board, and someone pulled that poll out from their backpack, and my friend Ana took a close look at it, and said, "Oh, no."

"What?" I said.

"I made a mistake on this," she said.

"What do you mean?"

"See here where it says, 'How would you describe your sexuality?' 'Homosexual' is listed first, and I checked that one off. I didn't even read it. I just went for what was first."

I thought it was funny, until the results were published in *The Crusader* a couple of weeks later. Of the respondents, two said they were homosexual. One of them was me, and one of them was Ana, who wasn't.

The Chaplain's Office, working off faulty intelligence, decided to put a support group together for the two students who were struggling with their sexual identity. I saw the ad right there in *The Crusader* a week later. That it was a support group, and not an activity group or a social group—that we were already being treated like we had a condition—didn't even faze me. What did was the possibility that there could be, despite mounting evidence to the contrary, more than one of us. Someone who had been too afraid to fill that questionnaire out. Someone who might sit with me on a couch and understand what I was talking about when I talk about this stuff. And then we'd make out.

It was too exciting to consider, and it was all I could consider.

I visited the Chaplain's Office and signed up for the first of what would be two separate interviews that I would have to go through to become a founding member of this group. They needed to talk to us all to make sure we weren't pranking them, or joining the group just to cause physical violence to gays and lesbians. It was sweet. I convinced them that I was serious—that I was so gay I didn't know what to do with myself—and was granted permission to attend the first meeting.

I was psyched.

On the day of the first meeting, I Sea Breezed my face, changed clothes seven times before settling on a simple Gap sweater and jeans—one doesn't want to appear overeager—and went. I took a deep breath, I opened the door, and inside the room sat one facilitator from the Chaplain's Office and three serious-looking starters from the Holy Cross women's field hockey team. I felt like someone who had won the wrong showcase in *The Price Is Right*'s Showcase Showdown. Like, I came here from Iowa, and now I have a Jet Ski.

The meeting was an even more somber affair than what you might expect from a roomful of skittish gay people and a Catholic priest. We were given copies of Brian McNaught's *On Being Gay* and urged to talk about our feelings. My feelings, quite frankly, were that I was tired of being scared. I wanted to be out. I wanted to be a beacon to other kids on campus, who I believed existed, who were searching for the same things. I wanted people to see that I was out and social and accepted and happy and that they could be too. I wanted them to find the inspiration to be brave and to live life as their truest self. Also, I wanted to have sex with dudes.

The women were warier, which in retrospect I understand. They were from tight, talky little New England, where if they were to come out publicly, their conservative families and friends from home might hear about it. They wanted to stay right where they were for the time being. Quickly, they proposed a policy: No talking to each other outside of the meeting. The women could talk to one another; they already knew each other and wouldn't need to invent a cover story. As for me, I was not to address any of them while we were outside the meeting place. It was too dangerous. I didn't like it, but I agreed.

After a couple months, facilitator Mary Pat called me in for a meeting. "We have a job for you," she told me. "There's a sophomore named Jeff who wants to join the group, but he's nervous about it." I perked all the way up. "We've met with him a few times, and I think he just needs to talk to someone who's been through it. Would you mind having coffee with him?" My heart pounded at the prospect of helping someone who was going through what I was still absolutely going through, and doubly so at her use of a male pronoun. I said that I would not mind having coffee with him. She said, "Great," and I said, "Terrific," and as I was about to leave, she said: "You should know this going in: Jeff is very, very handsome." *Of course he is,* I thought. I was already picturing him. Jeff had me long before hello.

Through Mary Pat, we arranged it. We chose a place off campus so as not to arouse suspicion, and a time when most of the student body was in class so as not to bump into anyone: Friday at 2:00. I buzzed with excitement and nerves and rage that I could not bend time to my will.

Friday at 2:00 finally came. I decided to be fashionably late, which is to say that I arrived at 2:01. Jeff was at a table, reading a book.

Jeff was beautiful.

Dark, wavy hair, the kind eyes and dimpled chin of a young Campbell Scott. He was *perfect*.

"Jeff?" I asked.

"Yeah, hi." He said. Nervous. Like me.

"I'm Dave." We shook hands. I felt it in the pit of my stomach. I felt a *handshake* in the pit of my stomach. "What are you reading?"

He held up the book and looked at the cover, and then at me. "I have no idea." And we laughed.

We talked about the school, and where he was from, and where I was from, and how weird it was that we were doing what we were doing. He mentioned how nervous he still was—he held up his hand about five minutes in and it was still shaking—and I tried to make him relax, to make it look like it was a real hoot to be a half-closeted gay guy at The College of the Holy Cross. I told him that of course he should totally come to the support group meeting, and also, funny enough, that I was having a party that very night and he should totally come to that, too. He said he would, and we said goodbye, and then I sprinted home to tell all of my friends and my roommate that we were having a party that night.

I'm going to play it cool, I told myself. *I'm not going to tell anyone what the deal is or how we met—I have to protect Jeff's anonymity, after all—I'm just going to take the opportunity to get to know him a little better.* He showed up a little later than everyone else—because I had told everyone else to show up an hour earlier than I told him to show up—and he was just as breathtaking as before, in a plaid, oversized Abercrombie & Fitch shirt. I greeted him with a red Solo tumbler and offered him "house cup" privileges, which allowed him to sail through the scrum around the keg, and we sat on the back of my couch, looking over the crowd and getting to know each other.

I told him I was in love with him roughly four minutes into this conversation.

I believe in love at first sight. I also believe that if you make someone repress their desire for love and companionship and sex for years and years during the time they need it the most, their hearts are like single cans of beer bouncing around the trunk of a car, and when someone comes along and fishes that can out and opens it, it makes a great big mess. Your first plausible shot at love feels a lot like your *only* plausible shot at love, and the longer you wait to have that first shot, the harder it is to tell them apart. Jeff and I were too young and inexperienced to know the difference. We thought we were in love and we kissed everywhere we were alone. Our rooms, elevators, stairways. Jeff came out to his roommate and a handful of friends. We were learning how to do this. Together.

We spent more or less every night in my bed, just holding each other. Nothing more. We were both afraid to go any further. Or I was, and he didn't want to. I didn't know. I didn't care. We were in a bubble, just me and Jeff, and everything was perfect. It felt like being out of control, and I loved it.

Here's how in love I felt: Michael Bolton's "Said I Loved You . . . But I Lied" was a hot one on the radio at the time, and I bought the cassette single. (The lie he teases in the title is that when he said he loved you, what he was actually feeling was *more than love*. Super-love. Extra-love. Bolton has been in the love bubble. Bolton *gets it*.)

The thing about bubbles is that they pop. After around three weeks, Jeff pulled his head out and realized that when two guys—especially when one of them is the one gay person on campus—are suddenly inseparable, people talk. There were suddenly *two* out gay people on campus, and without deciding to be one of them, Jeff had become one of them. The thing that had made him too nervous to attend a double-secret support group meeting only three weeks ago was suddenly something everyone might actually know. Also his boyfriend was a needy person who called fifty times a day and waited for him outside of class. Jeff did the only sensible thing and broke up with me.

He called me up and asked if I want to take a walk around campus, which is something we had done at his suggestion the day before, and I said sure, because all I wanted to do was spend time with him. And up on the landing of the administration building that overlooks the campus, he stopped and said: "Look, I'm sorry, but I can't do this anymore. I just can't. Do you understand that?" I said that I understood that, which I didn't, and that I'd been thinking we should cool it a little bit, too, which I hadn't. I said, "I know things are hard now, being here in this place, but I think we're good. You and I are good together. Maybe later? Maybe when we both graduate and we're out of here?" He was telling me it was over, and I was telling him I could accept that, as long as we could keep going. He said maybe, and we both knew he didn't mean it. I hugged him goodbye and I hopped in my car to go back to my apartment, and on the drive back, it hit me that he had called and asked to go for a walk around campus yesterday because he had wanted to break up with me yesterday, but he'd lost his nerve. That's the part that made me have to pull my car over and catch my breath.

At the next double-secret gay support group meeting, which I could not attend, because I could not face Jeff, two of the field hockey women revealed that I had broken our agreement and spoken to them outside of the meeting room, and that this had made them feel unsafe. Mary Pat called me and said I was not allowed to come back to the meetings, but that I could talk to her in private sessions if I wanted, and that since all of my transgressions had taken place in bars or at house parties at which I'd been drinking, I should seek alcohol counseling.

Jeff handled being out on campus like a champ. He ended up being kind of an inspiration to other kids who were going through the same thing. The support group grew and grew, and soon there was the stirring of a strong, vibrant community that I wasn't allowed to talk to.

And I became aware that I had fallen in love with a projection. When I tried to think about things I could say to Jeff to make it better, I couldn't think of any, and I couldn't think of any because I didn't know him. He was the first beautiful boy—one of my people, one of the people I was trying to be—who could conceivably love me back in the same way, and I'd decided to endow him with every trait I was looking for in a boyfriend, whether he had them or not. Whether he wanted them or not.

In retrospect, it's kind of like when you're auditioning for something and the casting person is behind schedule. You end up sitting in the waiting room for much longer than you expected to. And because there's nothing else to do—there's a

Coke machine and an old *USA Today* and the cell reception is shitty and there's no Wi-Fi—you start to get in your head. You get nervous about this thing that you usually do with ease. You read over your lines too many times. You think about what you're going to do with your hands. You think about what a gig like this one could do for you, what you'd do with the money. And when they finally call your name, you go in and just eat it. You talk too quickly, you talk too loudly, you oversell the joke in the script. You show the worst version of yourself. You want to run out of the place and never stop running. You've ruined it because you waited too long and you wanted it too much.

This was that kind of deal.

I threw all my love at a guy I barely knew, and it injured him. I wagged my tail so hard I knocked everything off the coffee table. The lucky thing was that this was happening right as Lisa Loeb and Nine Stories released their debut single "Stay (I Missed You)," which, by being plaintive and just vague enough, echoed my personal experience. I only heard what I wanted to, and I only wanted to hear that song, all day, every day.

Jeff and I never spoke again before I graduated, but I did make sure to ask all of his friends about him every time I saw them. One never knows when one is behaving like a creep; probably even that astronaut lady who drove for two days to beat up her ex-boyfriend's new girlfriend didn't think twice when she bought those adult diapers. It just felt right. Morrissey released the single "The More You Ignore Me, the Closer I Get" at just this moment—which I think you will agree is a very Morrissey thing to do—and it would have to join Suzanne Vega in the "listen later" pile.

That was a heavy couple of chapters. Thanks for sticking with me. As a reward, here is a photograph of a young Grant Show.

So You've Had Your Heart Broken in the '90s: A Playlist

I SPENT my whole college career, and then most of the rest of my twenties, loving guys who were either constitutionally incapable of loving me back or wise enough to keep their distance. It was a dumb, exquisitely painful, self-destructive pattern that I seemed to enjoy. If it never led to any romantic or sexual satisfaction for me, if I lived my life in a perpetual state of frustration and heartache, at least it was predictable. I was a lot of fun to be around in the '90s.

Here are a few of the songs that got me through it.

"Weak"—SWV

This one gets the early crush period down kind of perfectly; it's a physical trauma, an affliction, and one you don't want to shake off. You see a confident yet bookish senior pull out his word processor from across the library, you watch as he furrows his brow and taps away, and this song cues up in your soul. It's glorious. It makes you want to sing, even if you are in a quiet area. You can imagine yourself joining in this one, a capella, with Coko and the gals. You in a mock turtleneck and Cross Colours pants, them in doorknocker earrings and flannels casually tied about the waist, on a stoop in a rapidly gentrifying urban area. Afterwards you'll go for fudge!

"Where Does My Heart Beat Now"—Céline Dion

A hot bowl of cheese meant to be sung with a tear-choked voice and a freshly shattered heart. This one is so potent, so dramatic, they couldn't even find a good enough American singer to get it across. So they went up to Canada, taught Céline the lyrics phonetically, styled her like Elayne Boosler, and we were off to the races. For extra comfort, watch the video on YouTube and count all the times where she gesticulates on the wrong words.

"I'd Die Without You"—PM Dawn

PM Dawn gets lumped in with Digable Planets and Arrested Development and all those other early-'90s groups that pushed hip-hop into a gentler direction and then immediately fizzled out, but we forget that they wrote some fairly epic pop songs, and did it in caftans. Like all of their songs, this one is awash in hippie nonsense, but once you get to the chorus, you can sing along, and snap, and smoke, and cry. And repeat.

"Star Me Kitten"—R.E.M.

You will inevitably become confused and frustrated by the fact that your boy does not, maybe even cannot, love you back, and you will turn again to music. Yes, of course there is "Everybody Hurts," but anybody can be heartbroken to that one. You're special. Skip a few ahead on *Automatic for the People* until you get to this one, which is every bit as hangdog sad but, with its climactic "fuck me kitten," gives us a rare peek at Michael Stipe's horny side. At the height of my addiction to this song, I used to think about Todd, a viciously sexy and not particularly nice hockey player I hung out with for a while. I think he went on to be in the Army Special Forces. Todd was committed to hotness. (Incidentally, according to whatever magazines I was reading, Michael Stipe was hanging out with Stephen Dorff a lot in the mid-'90s, so he knows about intense crushes on sexy idiots.)

"Larry"—Buffalo Tom

That whole Buffalo Tom *Let Me Come Over* album, really. I don't know about you, but when I hear "Larry," I am running toward whomever I have a crush on, and he is running toward me, in the pouring rain, and then we are kissing. It is possible that I am living inside a WB young-adult show, even now.

"Desperately Wanting"—Better Than Ezra

Sometimes you don't have to know all the words for a song to be your go-to heartbreak anthem. Sometimes it just has to have a title like "Desperately Wanting," and a part in the chorus after a bunch of words you haven't bothered to learn where the lead singer sings the words "desperately wanting," and you can shout it along with him—because you too are desperately wanting. He understands. You are on the same page, you and whatever the guy's name is from Better Than Ezra.

"The Freshmen"—The Verve Pipe

Oh, who even knows what this one is about. It's just kind of moody and plodding and "we were merely freshmen" is a great excuse for unwise romantic fixations, even when you're twenty-eight. Plus, for a moment, the goddamn thing was inescapable; it seems wasteful not to use it as the soundtrack to a self-destructive crush.

Literally Anything by Toad the Wet Sprocket

Were these guys ever happy? I picture them all in windbreakers, on a late autumn afternoon, just having finished crying. Every song is about one single person bravely dealing with some agonizing thing, or standing stalwart in the face of a chill wind, or putting on a smile while inside they're aching, just aching, and when you're young and you love torturing yourself, it is exactly what you need to hear.

"Elderly Woman Behind the Counter in a Small Town"—Pearl Jam

A potent reminder that, no matter how intense the one-way fixation is, how hot and focused the love beams you're shooting out of your eyes are, or how perfect everything would be if he could just feel a tiny bit of the same about you as you do about him, hearts and thoughts they fade, fade away. It'll all pass in a few weeks and you'll be on to the next one. You and SWV will be back harmonizing over Fruitopias before you know it.

7

Free Your Mind

M Y SENIOR YEAR OF COLLEGE, I WAS THE CAMPUS SO-
cial chair, because I loved to throw parties and also nobody gets more done than a young person who is furiously
sublimating his need for intimacy. And so it was that in the
summer of 1993, I was sent to a student leadership conference
at Emory University in Atlanta, where something happened to
me that you are not going to believe, but that I swear to God is
absolutely true.

That summer, incidentally, was the one where I had decided
I would come out to my family. I was still somewhere between
partially and completely out at school, and since I'd already
more or less decided I wouldn't be coming back to St. Louis
after graduation, it would be the last time we'd spend more
than a few days together. And how better to celebrate your last
summer with your parents than by making an announcement
that forces them, for at least a few brief moments, to picture
you having sex?

I came home in late May, set down my bags, saw their smiling faces, and mentally dragged and dropped this task from
early June to very, very late August. Oh, sure, I meant to sit
them down and say something, but we were having such a nice
time. I oscillated wildly between an honest desire for them not

to hear about it from someone else, to a very real wish that someone else would hurry up and tell them. I didn't know what to do, and I didn't have anyone to tell me what to do, so I did nothing.

In mid-August, I hopped on a plane to Atlanta to spend three days with some other student leaders from around the country at this conference. This being the early 1990s, political correctness was in full bloom, and this event would focus on programming functions that would reflect our culture's growing diversity. As conservative and homogeneous as my college and hometown were, I imagined this conference as a Utopia filled with different types of people, all mutually respecting one other; a really sexy Benetton ad. Whatever doubts I had about myself and my looming announcement would simply melt away under the stern eye of our retreat leaders: tough-but-caring Lou Gossett Jr. types who'd beat some pride and self-reliance into me, to the point where I'd hardly be able to wait to get home and tell my parents the good news. The informational brochure arrived a week or so before the event and revealed that the conference would be titled "Diversity: Isn't That Special?" I had a bad feeling, and I immediately got to work repressing it.

The registration table was directly underneath the giant diversity: isn't that special? banner, and I signed my papers and received my room assignment as Arrested Development's "People Everyday" bumped out of the ballroom's PA system. Just when I was finishing up, Debi, a pantsuited administrator with a fanny pack and a harsh attempt at the Chynna Phillips/ Jane from *Melrose Place* hairdo, fixed her eyes on me with a look of practiced disapproval. "Blue eyes," she sneered. "We know all about people like you. *Go sit on the floor.*" I'm more hazel, but the distinction didn't seem important, so I went and sat on the floor next to a beefy lacrosse type in a Clemson T-shirt. "Hello," said Clemson. "Welcome to a clumsy parable about racism." "They *wouldn't*," I said, as a Hispanic girl from Vassar was led to a table where a group of brown-eyed people ate steak and baked potatoes. They would. They *are*.

And so it continued: all the brown-eyed people were shown to tables and given fancy meals, while all of the blond girls in topknots—and in the tradition of student leadership conferences, this thing was roughly 94 percent blond girls in topknots—were sent to huddle on the floor and share those packets of orange crackers with peanut butter in between. Clemson and I watched blonde after blonde hit the deck and scan the room in frustration, thinking something must be the matter, minds getting primed to be blown. A blue-eyed Janeane Garofalo type from UVA plopped herself down next to us. "Racism's bad news, huh? Gimme a cracker."

After all the conference attendees were accounted for, and right when we were speculating as to whether they'd lead the blue-eyed people outside and turn a fire hose on us, Debi took the stage. "Oh, here it comes," said UVA. Debi's voice fought with the feedback for a moment: "Welcome to 'Diversity: Isn't That Special?' Now, you might have noticed that some of you have been treated differently than others."

"Yep, got that," said Clemson as a murmur passed over the floor.

"Doesn't feel too good, does it?" Debi continued.

"Oh, it's awful," I whispered.

"Well, that's because we . . ."

". . . are doing a thing about racism," we said.

". . . have taught you kind of a sneaky lesson . . ."

". . . about racism."

". . . *about racism.*" The murmur grew to a roar. Blond ponytails bobbed this way and that. "See, some of you, just because of the color of your eyes, had a completely different experience than your neighbors, and you may not even have known why." The room was in a full uproar. The topknots simply could not take this information in. "See, racism is still alive and well in this country, and some people like to judge other people on the color of their skin. *It's not fair, is it?*" The brown-eyed kids at the tables, many of whom were black or Hispanic and had therefore, as minority student leaders, probably been forced to endure at least one of these simulations before, mostly shrugged and finished up their baked potatoes. "You are free to introduce yourselves to one another. Talk about what you've learned."

The topknots made a beeline for the black kids, with speeds that tested the integrity of their scrunchies. "Is this what it's like for you?" "You guys, I am so sorry!" "Can I touch your hair?" Baby steps toward enlightenment.

"Diversity: Isn't That Special?" continued along these lines. The next day, we were given a standardized test comprised largely of questions about jazz and basketball, to illustrate the cultural bias of the SAT. Too bad for Debi and her people, I was deep into an Afro-centric, Tribe Called Quest-inspired phase that summer, and had a huge crush on a college friend who talked a lot about sports, so I scored a 1540. The topknots got their poor numbers back, learned the point of the exercise, and shook their heads *no* with faces of steely determination. *Have you heard about this systemic racism?* their faces said. *Well, we just did, and it's bad.*

Right around here was the first time I ever even began to view my homosexuality as an asset rather than a liability. Maybe if I came out to some of these administrators, they'd view me as less of an oppressor. Maybe if I let them know I was actually a minority too, we could actually have a constructive talk about what I was going through, in real time, right then. So in a small-group discussion about sensitivity to gay and lesbian issues (alas, the *B* and the *T* were not yet invited to the party), I piped up: "You know, I'm actually gay myself, so . . ." and the facilitator squinted her eyes, made her lips disappear, tilted her head at a perfect 45-degree angle—the international symbol for You Poor Thing—and interrupted me. "So brave," she stage-whispered, and then got right back to her spiel about campus safer-sex programs. It went that way with each facilitator I came out to: the squint, the lips, the 45-degree head tilt. No dialogue, no "How are you?", no inquiry as to whether anything they were saying was resonating in any meaningful way, just a condescending look. I was being treated like a box of fragile glass figurines, or Cousin Geri from *The Facts of Life*.

The more sensitive among us hadn't really learned any constructive ways to vent our negative emotions in 1993; *Jagged Little Pill* was still two years off. Instead, Clemson, UVA, and I chose to express our frustrations through the medium of drinking. There was an Applebee's across the street from campus, and once things got too much, one of us would give the high sign—index finger making quick circles in the air— and one by one we'd disappear. We'd grab a table on the patio and smoke cigarettes and laugh and drink things that were blue. I came out to them, and they said "Okay," and we talked about it a little bit and then got on with what we'd been talking about, which for the record is exactly the way it's supposed to go. By accident, this conference was teaching us all something.

There was a farewell banquet on the evening of the third day, and as student leaders of all eye colors finished up their steak and potatoes, the administrators fired up a slide projector. And there it was, up on the silver screen: a greatest-hits compilation from "Diversity: Isn't That Special?" Slide after slide of white girls crying on patient brown shoulders, set to carefully selected hits of the day: "Free Your Mind" by En Vogue, "A Whole New World" by Peabo Bryson and Regina Belle, and then, finally: "What's So Funny About Peace, Love and Understanding."

Except it was the version from the soundtrack to *The Bodyguard*.

The Curtis Stigers version.

Oh, *hell* no.

Listen: you can condescend to me. You can cut me off and treat me like an injured baby bird when I try to start a dialogue with you. But don't you dare think you have anything to teach me if you don't know who Elvis Costello is.

I gave the high sign, and Clemson and UVA were headed for the door before my finger could complete a full rotation.

By our second round, the blue drinks started doing their job and our tongues were loosened, to the point where Clemson leaned forward and asked a question I'd waited a lifetime to hear: "Are you okay?"

"Yeah, no. Yeah," I answered, out of habit. "I'm fine."

And then I took a deep breath. "No. You know what, guys? I'm not okay. That was bullshit." My new friends nodded. "We spent three days talking about sensitivity and diversity, when I am right here being diverse and needing some sensitivity and nobody's letting me say anything. I am about to come out to my fucking family, which is scary, and I would love it if just one person in my fucking life would listen to me." People started to look over, because I was loud, and I didn't care. "I cannot be the only person in this world who's gone through this fucking problem. I do not need to be told how brave I am, I do not need the head at the 45-degree angle." Clemson and UVA gave a puzzled look, but chose to let me continue releasing steam. "I need what you and you and everyone I know has always had, and has never had to worry about not having, and that's someone they respect who has been through what they're going through, who can sit them down and tell them they're okay, and listen to what they have to say, and *tell them what to fucking do*. I am alone, and I am *furious*, and I am *scared to fucking death*, and I just want someone who isn't an idiot who's gone through this to

Tell.

Me.

What.

To.

Do."

We are now at the part of the story that you are not going to believe, but again: this actually happened.

I sat back in my wrought-iron patio seat, wiped my eyes, and lit a Marlboro Light. "That's it," I exhaled. "I just want someone to tell me what to do."

These words left my mouth, and in the very next second the door opened, and out onto the patio of the Applebee's across

from Emory University in Atlanta, Georgia, walked The Indigo Girls.

The.

Indigo.

Girls.

And not The Indigo Girls and their friends. Not The Indigo
Girls and their manager and publicist. Just The Indigo Girls.
Just Amy and Emily, taking time out to enjoy some boneless
wings with their choice of sauce.

It was as though they had seen some kind of gay distress
signal in the Atlanta skies and reported for duty. They sat
down at the table next to us. My jaw did not so much drop as
unhinge. The Blue Curaçao was really pumping through my
bloodstream, so I did not hesitate to turn to my left and start
in:

"Um . . . Amy? Yeah, hi, my name's Dave and I'm gay just
like you and I'm sort of about to come out to my family and see
I'm here for this conference and I tried to talk but they do the
angle and they don't know who Elvis Costello is and . . ."

"You know what," she stopped me, "I'm Emily."

"Sorry!" I gritted my teeth and sucked in air. "That happens a lot probably, right?"

"Not really," said Emily. "But I get you. Been there. Coming out is hard, and it's something you have to do on your
own. You gotta trust yourself." She patted my knee. "You're
okay. Just trust yourself." And then she turned to Amy and
got down to the business of choosing an Appeteaser, her work
having been done.

And I'll be damned if that wasn't the best advice I'd ever
gotten. I flew home to St. Louis the next day and stood face-
to-face with my parents and took a deep breath and immedi-

ately waited a couple more weeks and then came out to them. It was awful, and it took some time for things to be okay, but they were, eventually. I trusted myself, and I got through it.

I went back to school, ready to spend my fifth year pros-trate to the higher mind, get my paper, and, finally, be free.

8

I'll Be There for You

AS GRADUATION LOOMED, I DECIDED THAT I NEEDED to escape the Holy Cross of my mind. Enough of small places where everyone knows each other, enough of homogeneity. I was going to move to the biggest, greatest city in the world: I was starting over in New York City. I had enthusiasm, a poor understanding of how the world worked, a 2.4 GPA, and no job skills. I couldn't fail.

In the spring semester of my senior year, I started sending out cover letters and résumés to advertising agencies in New York. I decided that Madison Avenue was the place for me: There was creativity, proximity to media, and suspenders, plus, a lifetime of pretending everything was fine when it wasn't would seem to make me a natural.

A few agencies got back to me to set up interviews, the first of which was Saatchi & Saatchi in SoHo. I drove down from campus and spent the night at the Best Western in the South Street Seaport. And as is customary when I travel, I forgot one major item. Sometimes it's a basic thing like toothpaste or deodorant; this time it was socks. I had a brand-new, early graduation present Brooks Brothers suit, which without socks would simply be too jaunty. Unacceptable. My interview was at 9:00 a.m., and so, bright and early, I hunted the Seaport for a pair of socks. Nothing. All that was open was a Walgreens, and their offerings were limited, but I was a hosiery beggar and therefore could not choose. I grabbed, I paid, I donned, I ran.

And so it was that I received my first big-boy job offer while wearing a gray, glen plaid suit and opaque women's black thigh-high drugstore stockings.

I accepted. I got back in my car for the drive back to campus and Z100 was playing Collective Soul's "Shine." My new life had begun. I was an ad guy now. And a L'Eggs gal. Heaven, let your light shine down.

I began looking for apartments right away. My perception of New York apartments and their size came mostly from Janet Jackson's "Pleasure Principle" video and *Big:* I envisioned massive, untreated warehouse spaces with floor-to-ceiling windows and exposed pipes. The heavy-doored elevator would open right into my place. I'd wait a tasteful few months before getting a trampoline.

The first place I saw was an $800/month jail cell in Chelsea with no kitchen or bathroom, shown to me by an angry man of indeterminate ethnic origin in a tank top. "Is shared bathroom. Is New Jork, is always shared bathroom. You sign liss? I am very busy." I gave that guy a firm maybe and kept looking, settling on a place on the Upper East Side, right above Elaine's on Second Avenue. It had wood floors at a 15-degree angle, so that if you opened the refrigerator, you had to keep a hand on the top of the unit so that it wouldn't topple and crush you.

I signed the lease, bought a pillow and a blanket from Bed Bath & Beyond, and stayed the night. New York City! As night fell, I decided to go see what was what, the only way

I knew how: by hailing a taxi, getting into the backseat, and telling the cabdriver: "I'm new here. Take me somewhere gay and awesome."

What was cool was that he didn't stab and rob me. Instead, he broke it down. Fahad had been there for sixteen years and he told me: "It's going to be hard to live here at first, but after a few weeks, you won't be able to live anywhere else." I believed him. He dropped me at a West Village bar called The Monster that was apparently popular with Middle Eastern gay men at the time, wished me luck, and sent me on my way. I made some new friends there, tourists whom I accompanied to the Duplex for cabaret, where I met people who took me to Squeezebox at Don Hill's to dance to punk music with drag queens. There I met people who brought me up to Club USA, where I made out with someone after talking to him for five minutes, and then rode "The K-Hole," a three-story slide whose name I was too green to understand. It was an adventure. It was what I was moving to New York for.

I stumbled out of Club USA into a sunny summer Saturday morning, raised my arm to hail a taxi home, and—I'm not joking—Fahad pulled up.

"Well?" he asked.

"I love it."

I never had the same cabdriver twice again in the eight years I lived there. My first real night in the city made it seem ordained, like God wanted me to be there.

It got a lot less glamorous, pretty much right away.

+ + +

When you live in New York City and you have an entry-level job and you are in your early twenties, you know every draft beer and chicken wing special in town. This is how you feed yourself, physically and emotionally. You meet and make your friends in these places because you are all there for the same reason. Every bar on the Upper East Side of Manhattan is a singles bar where all of the singles are also interviewing potential friends. Everyone is twenty-two and fresh out of college, missing a dining hall with a meal program, or their fraternity brothers or sorority sisters, or their actual families. Everyone is at the bottom of the corporate ladder and has been hollered at earlier in the day by a boss who is twenty-seven. Everyone has big plans and nice new clothes and a little bit—a very little bit—of folding money. Everyone wants to find the people who'll be there for them.

This is what *Friends* gets right about living in cities in your twenties: for at least a little while, you live as a tribe. You're out of your parents' house, and you're not yet settled down with a spouse and kids and a house in the suburbs, but you still need family. You still need to feel like you belong to something. So you pull a family unit together out of what you find in the places you haunt. You have your hangout where you meet to complain about work. You date people and run them past your friends. You have keys to one another's apartments, and then you move in together. You travel as a pack.

My official move to New York happened in the summer of 1994, and by the time *Friends* premiered that September, my posse was tight. We rolled six deep, just like on the show. I saw myself as the Chandler of the group, but in a time before *BuzzFeed* quizzes it was difficult to know for sure.

The gang started coming together right away. I drove down to New York the day after I graduated, with my parents in a rental Buick right behind me. They moved me in and bought me a Jennifer Convertible and some pots, pans, and plates, and together we furnished my three-hundred-square-foot home. They got me settled and told me that their last graduation present to me would be to drive my car out of the city and back to St. Louis. (I didn't understand why that was a present and not theft, and they told me: "Wait." Sure enough, by the end of my first week, I was grateful not to be burdened with an automobile in New York City; I could barely afford to park my body there.) We said goodbye and all of our chins trembled but we kept it together. "Three to five years," I told my mother. "Three to five and then I'm back in St. Lou." And they got in the cigarette-reeking Jetta with the front bumper duct-taped on, and I watched my car and the two people I loved the most in the world chug down Second Avenue, getting smaller and smaller as my youth receded into the distance. I wanted to cry, but I am Catholic and Irish, so I started drinking.

It was around 4:00 p.m., and the few acquaintances I knew in the city were still at work, so I went to my local bodega to buy a stack of tabloids—the *New York Post* would be my tabloid of record at last, with a dash of the free weekly *New York Press* for when I was feeling intellectual and contrarian—and took myself to Kelley's Korner, a pub at the northwest corner of Eighty-ninth and Second. It was completely empty. After thirty minutes or so, after I'd managed to read about every MURDER HACK and PSYCHO GALPAL and made an honest attempt to learn the names of the good socialites of the moment, a woman about my age walked in. A Jewish beauty with a "Prove Your Love"–era Taylor Dayne mane seated herself a few stools down with her own stack of reading materials. A *Daily News* and *Village Voice* kind of gal, she was. It was just the three of us: bartender in Yankees T-shirt, Taylor

Dayne, and me, as Seal played in the background. (When you are drinking in the early '90s and the sun is up, Seal is always playing in the background. Especially at brunches. To this day, if you play me "A Prayer for the Dying," my body will naturally point toward the nearest source of hollandaise sauce. Ditto for Crash Test Dummies' "God Shuffled His Feet" and "Bamboleo" by the Gipsy Kings.)

Finally, the bartender spoke up. "Okay, you two have to start talking to each other." We agreed. Her name was Alicia; she was just starting a gig at The Food Network; and she, too, was waiting for her friends to get out of work. We made the bartender, Johnny, fire up the NTN bar trivia machine, and we faced off in movie trivia. She did not stand a chance, but she was a good sport. Afterward, I invited her up to my place, which was basically upstairs and furnished with only my CD boom box and my steamer trunk full of mixtapes and CDs. We were young and open and confident that the other was not a murder hack or a psycho galpal, and we listened to the *Reality Bites* soundtrack and talked about ourselves. We've been friends ever since.

The group grew from there. A few days later, we grabbed happy hour at The Launch—a place up on Third Avenue that sold $2 cheeseburger and french-fry platters before it was troublingly shut down by the Board of Health—and were seated next to Louise, a refined New Jersey girl with British parents, and Aimee, a wild-haired New Orleans debutante with a massive smile, a ready laugh, and the tolerance of a girl who grew up in New Orleans. After a few $5 pitchers of happy-hour draft beer, our conversations overlapped, and then our two-tops joined into a four, our phone numbers changed hands, and it was *on*. Soon after, a female friend from college went out on a date with a prepster from Philadelphia's main line and brought him by The Launch to show him off, where he hit on me kind of unabashedly, and thereby I lost a female friend from college and gained an on-and-off boyfriend named Jim. My friend Mike from high school moved to New York because he did a thing called "writing code" and got a job at Sony working on something called their "website." (He brought me to his office one Saturday afternoon, just to show me what the Internet was. He directed me to "Yahoo!," and said: "Search for anything. I bet there's a website for it." I searched for *Small Wonder*. There were eight websites devoted to *Small Wonder* reminiscence, memorabilia, and fan fiction. There was never a time when the Internet wasn't ridiculous.)

We showed up at one another's apartment parties that were impenetrably crowded if more than nine people showed up. We made runs to Key Food for Top Ramen together. There were six of us, and if we were not at work we were together in one configuration or another, but mostly all six. We went to Pedro's on Ninety-second, with the frayed college pennants lining the walls. In wintertime, we sat by the fire at Dorrian's, the place where the Preppie Murderer met his Murder Galpal, playing euchre and drinking ourselves warm. In the summertime, we'd rollerblade around Central Park and meet in the Sheep Meadow to divide up the Sunday *New York Times* and buy the Budweiser tallboys the hustlers sold out of garbage bags for one dollar.

When our direct deposits showed up in our accounts and we were flush, we'd walk down to JG Melon for burgers. We largely skipped movies, because they ate into our happy hour budgets, but we managed to see *Pulp Fiction* at the Angelica, with the N/R line rumbling beneath our seats at the crucial adrenaline-shot scene. We wore Brooks Brothers shirts or Ann Taylor sweater sets with heavy, thick-soled boots, and we thought about getting our eyebrows pierced, but we never did.

We chose our clubhouse: The Gaf, a tiny place on 83rd with a good jukebox, which is to say a CD jukebox with Oasis's *Definitely Maybe* and the first G. Love and Special Sauce, and space for no more than fifteen people. We developed crushes on bartenders up and down 1st Avenue. (Louise malapropped the perfect word for this, while trying to say *bartender* and *boyfriend* at the same time: *barfriender.*) We met at brunch and acquired appetites for Bloody Marys and pieced together our Saturday nights over Eggs Benedict and let our waitresses sit down with us for a moment because they were inevitably as hung over as we were.

We were, as Des'ree commanded, bad and bold and wiser. We were young New Yorkers. We went to each other's restaurants—all of us except Louise, who worked on Wall Street, had second jobs at restaurants, because we were all entry-level and the rent, even then, was too damn high—and we comped each other's meals. Aimee picked up the weekend breakfast shift at The Barking Dog up on Third; I served schnitzel to New York's German community at the Yorkville Inn on Second.

I had never waited tables before, but I fabricated a long résumé of restaurant work because I needed the money. I was twice as inept a waiter as I was an ad guy; I would bring you the wrong thing always, and you would never get water or salt, but I knew how to make conversation, so I held on for a few months. And then one night, I showed a young couple to their table and handed them their menus, which were made of paper, over a lit candle. His survived, but hers caught the flame and began to smolder on the upper right corner. I said, with the practiced calm of a young advertising person who doesn't want anyone to know he has no idea what he's doing: "Pardon me, ma'am, your menu is on fire," and I took it back, stamped it out, and got her a new one. My manager watched this with wide eyes and I nodded at her, and at the end of my shift I silently turned in my apron and that was that.

At any time of the day or night, I could tell you where the other five of these people were. We were in constant contact, which in 1994 required effort. We had no cell phones or e-mail or Instant Messager; we could not text one another; and as Julie's behavior toward Heather B. in the first episode of *The Real World* so memorably demonstrated, beepers were mostly for drug dealers. Keeping tabs on one another meant calling and leaving messages on one another's answering machines, which, if you had an upscale model, would allow you to check your messages remotely from your desk or a phone booth, with a four-digit security code. There were no emojis or even emoticons; if you wanted to wink at someone you had to actually wink *right at them in real life,* which is a thing we can all agree is gross. We were forced to interact in real life. And because we didn't know any better, we loved it.

* * *

It was good that I was rarely alone, because I did stupid things when I was alone. Once, after a work happy hour that turned into a legitimate barhop in the West Village, I got up, did the Irish goodbye, and began my long journey home: West Village to the Upper East Side, a three-trainer, exhausting under the best of circumstances. I hopped on the 1 to Forty-second, took the shuttle to Grand Central, and got on the northbound 6 headed for Eighty-sixth and Lexington. At Seventy-seventh, the train pulled into the station and the doors swung open, and then it just stayed there for a while, like New York trains are known to do. The train had stopped due to congestion ahead, or something of that nature; I'd have to walk the last ten or so blocks. I got out of the train to do that, just as an idea slunk through the fog of my brain: What if I *don't* walk home on the street? The tunnel is right there, *what if I go through it on foot?*

What if I walk through a subway tunnel at 3 a.m.? (That's how stupid I was in my twenties: I didn't have a ready answer for the question *What if I walk through a subway tunnel at 3 a.m.?*)

There was a narrow walkway the same height of the subway platform, and it ran as far up as I could see, so I took it. I walked until the light from the Seventy-seventh Street platform faded away and it was pitch dark, and then I kept walking. Somehow it kept getting darker. I was alone at 3:00 a.m. in a subway tunnel. I walked until I couldn't even see a pinhole of light in front of or behind me. I was so scared I passed scared and came back around to calm, the way you get when you skydive. Except unlike skydiving, you can actually really die when you're alone in a dark subway tunnel, and it would be a much more difficult death to explain to your parents.

For reasons I cannot explain, exploring felt like the thing to do. I came upon a stairway and walked a few steps down it, and then I heard skittering. Not the skittering of rodent feet; sadly, by this time I was able to identify that noise. No, this was *people* skittering. This was the noise of *tunnel people*. These were CHUDs or drug addicts or CHUDs who were addicted to a drug that is derived from human flesh. These people might kill me, or eat me alive, or pull me down to become their mother. Whichever, respectfully: no thanks. I ran back up to walkway level and broke into a dead sprint toward Eighty-sixth.

By this time, the train had started running again. The conductor was at the front, at the controls, and his headlight fell right on me. I turned around and stuck out a thumb. Like: Can you *believe* what I'm doing right now? He could not believe what I was doing right then. He put his hands out to either side of his head, the international sign for *What. The. Fuck?*, and stared at me, stupefied, as he passed. I ran all the way to the Eighty-sixth Street station and onto the platform, sprinting up the stairs past the police and the station agent, and all the way home. On the way, I passed the Yorkville Inn, where I had waited tables and acquired a fairly solid reputation as an idiot. A few of my co-workers were there, and my body was flush with adrenaline; I wanted to tell them what I'd done. My old coworker Eamonn looked at me and said: "David. Go to the bathroom." I said I didn't have to go to the bathroom, I had to tell them a story. He said: *"David. Go to the bathroom."* So I did, and I looked at myself in the mirror. I was covered head to toe in subway tunnel soot. I was in blackface. I was a *mess*.

I told the rest of my gang that story over brunch the next day, slightly proud of myself. A few hours later Aimee called me and said: "We talked about your story for a while after you left, and we all agreed it was the dumbest thing we've ever heard a human being do." I couldn't argue.

This is the moment when I had the conscious thought, for the first time in my life: "Maybe I shouldn't *actively try to kill myself* anymore."

It was Louise who ended up giving me the second half of

the wake-up call I needed. We were talking about what she looked for in a boyfriend, and her first and least-flexible requirement was that he love what he does for a living. It startled me. "Really?"

"Yes, of course. It's what you spend most of your life doing, so it should be a thing you're in love with."

It's a simple, undeniable truth, and I can't believe I didn't hear someone say it out loud until I was well into my twenties. Though it was never said to me this way explicitly, I'd come to regard work as a thing that must be endured, a pain in the neck, a thing you *offer up t'Are Lard*. We even treat business and pleasure as separate travel categories, as though they can't be the same thing. As though to be a man in full, it was my responsibility to put on a necktie, disappear for ten hours a day, and then come home and not talk much about it, just as my father had, just as his father had.

"Do"—I was stunned by this new concept—"do *you* love what you do?"

"Of course I do. I can't wait to go to work in the morning." It was like finding out one of your closest friends can levitate, or is Mormon. My world was shaken. I was suddenly self-conscious about the idea that I didn't love what I did, and I wasn't particularly good at it besides. And I was a little hurt because I kind of assumed she spent her whole workday counting the minutes until we could all be together again, the way I did.

Louise saved my life with one offhand comment. You do that to each other when you're twenty-five.

In a separate conversation, Louise gave me another life lesson: if your office has one of those massive toilet paper rolls in the stalls, and if you can work a fingernail or a coin into the center screw of the dispenser, you can take the cover off and turn the roll into a kind of pillow for an early-afternoon nap. "Just put your forehead right on it. You can get a good fifteen minutes that way, and sometimes that's all you need."

I put the second lesson to work right away. The first one took a few years to digest.

What We Talk About When We Talk About the '90s

MAN, I miss the 1990s. I mean, I'm very happy now, but I'm also exhausted and sore and furious at everyone who disagrees with me even a little bit about anything, and I find myself pining for a simpler time. Nineties nostalgia is at a fever pitch at the moment, and while we're naturally a little misty-eyed for things that happened twenty years ago, I think it's about more than that. I think we left something there, something we can't get back. Here are a few of those things.

Optional Snark

In the 1990s, if you wanted to look down your nose at something, you could relax, because Janeane Garofalo was available to do it for you. Snark, a particularly cutting brand of sarcasm or irony, was a thing to be deployed by smart people: David Letterman, *Spy Magazine*, the people who wrote the Dubious Achievement Awards for *Esquire*. Then David Spade brought it to the masses with SNL's "Hollywood Minute," blogs and social media were invented, and now even children are over everything.

As for Janeane, she had her lips done and got herself a Bravo scripted series. As ever, she is one step ahead of us all.

Teen Shows That Were Earnest

Those Salinger kids in *Party of Five* dealt with some real drama—dead parents, alcoholism, dating a guy who ends up being kind of racist—and they faced it head-on and wet-eyed. *Saved by the Bell* may have been watched ironically, but they made that shit with a straight face. I don't even have the emotional fortitude to address *Blossom* and her very special episodes. For a moment there, we seemed to believe that television was a way to change hearts and minds, and that the best way to do it was to be emotionally direct and kind of embarrassing. Nowadays, the *90210* kids would have to murder one another graphically every week and all talk like the same twenty-three-year-old gay guy who's trying too hard.

The Feeling That Anything Could Happen, Radio-Wise

Nirvana blew everything wide open in the early '90s, and radio jumped on the "alternative" bandwagon, looking for the next big thing. They didn't find it, but we got a few years of truly excellent one-hit wonders: New Radicals, Primitive Radio Gods, The Toadies; even the Butthole Surfers and the Meat Puppets had hits. You turned on commercial radio not knowing what you were going to hear next. Now you hear all of these songs on Jack FM in between Mariah Carey and Meat Loaf.

Black Guys in Pastels

Say what you will about their overreliance on vocal runs, but Boyz II Men could rock a mauve.

Unreachability

If you wanted to e-mail someone, you went home, turned on your computer and modem, fired up Prodigy, waited a half-hour for it to load, and then said something that was worthy of your effort. The rest of the time, you existed in the actual world. You looked where you were going. You were alone sometimes. And you didn't think you'd ever be nostalgic for it.

An Internal Life

The other day, I had a thought about something, and as is now my reflex, I reached for my phone to tweet it. And I don't know what stopped me—maybe I was heading down into a subway station or something—but for some reason, I stopped. I thought: this thought will have to stay inside my head, unexpressed. A feeling of calm washed over me. It was the first time I'd done that since late 2006.

9

Show Me Love

ONE SUNDAY NIGHT WHEN I WAS ELEVEN, I FLIPPED
through the channels for something to watch, and I rested
on PBS, because there were robots on it. And thus began my
brief but intense love affair with *Doctor Who*. The show hit all
my buttons: it was sci-fi, it was British, and I was the only one
I knew who had heard of it. Plus, it was all so charmingly low-
budget. It felt like it needed me. I became a fan right away.

After I'd been watching for a few months, the station ran
a promo for a "*Doctor Who* and *Star Trek* Convention" down
at the St. Louis Art Museum. *What.* I begged my parents to
drive me down there and drop me off for the day. I was sure
it would be packed with people my age, people who wandered
their schools feeling like half a circle. People who were waiting
for me the way I'd been waiting for them.

My parents relented, and we drove the half-hour downtown.
I got there right as the doors opened at 10 a.m., and told my
folks: "Pick me up at five." I went inside and, well, it was full
of what I now recognize as the kinds of grown-ups who would
willingly have gone to *Doctor Who* and *Star Trek* conventions
in 1982: adults with long Tom Baker scarves and Captain Kirk
costumes, or pointed ears, or i grok spock T-shirts. Or all of it.

I remember saying to myself "Oh, *hell* no."

The attendees weren't much kinder to me, for what it's worth. I was the youngest person there by a decade or more, and people gave me looks. Like: *We have come to dress like space lords and talk to each other in Klingon; what on Earth is a* child *doing here?*

I made the best of it for as long as I could, sat through a screening of *The Trouble with Tribbles* that the entire audience recited line for line, and then gave up and called home, begging my parents to pick me up.

Twelve years later, this would basically be the story of my first few gay bar experiences in New York.

*   *   *

In 1994, the biggest of the big gay bars in New York City was a place called Splash on Nineteenth Street in the eastern reaches of Chelsea. I had learned this from *The Village Voice,* which in my last few weeks of college I studied more closely than any textbook. The clubs—Twilo, the Roxy, the Tunnel—were out of the question, as a $30 cover charge was not in my budget, so I wrote down the address for Splash and made a plan to hit it on my first Friday.

The countdown to the end of that first Friday was endless; I watched the clock at Saatchi & Saatchi like Britney would, years later, at the beginning of the "Baby One More Time" video. At 5:00 p.m. on the dot, I ran out the door. I didn't even go home to have a spritz of Drakkar Noir and put on a casual button-down; there was just no time. My people were waiting. I threw open the doors, and, as was required by local ordinance at the time, Robin S's "Show Me Love" was playing. The place was jam-packed. Go-go boys in speedos taking showers in glass cases. Videos of gay pride parades of old playing on the video monitors. And as I ordered a beer and scanned the crowd, I began to notice something. The boys were . . . oddly similar. Short hair, lots of product, styled forward. Tank tops, tight. Jeans, tight. They even had the same shoulders. I had never seen such uniformity, and I had spent six years at a boys' school with a dress code.

Once I had downed the two beers necessary for striking up a conversation with a stranger, I picked a handsome guy who was standing alone at the other end of the room. My attempts to make eye contact were not working out, so I walked over and extended my hand. "Hi! I'm Dave." He scanned me from head to toe.

"No, thanks."

I have a theory. I think everybody needs to join a club at some point in his or her life. People have a natural hunger to be on the inside, and the later they satisfy that hunger, the more of a nightmare person they turn into. Take fraternities and sororities: a person who has fit in somewhere before having joined a fraternity tends to put the experience in its proper place, while a person for whom it's their first club tends to take it way too seriously. Similarly, if a person gets through college without ever having been on the inside, and then moves to a big city and is immediately accepted into the gay community, he has a tendency to be the worst. He learns the rules and the lingo and the dress code, and he is fucking vicious to the people who don't know them. He has been denied membership in a club until very late in life, and *someone is going to pay.*

In the gay male community of New York City in 1994, the fat guy was the someone who paid. It was not yet cool to be a hefty, scruffy gay dude the way it is now. Gay men have always been a little more body-conscious than the rest of the population; guys are visual and sexual and disgusting and hot, after all. But in the years after the initial AIDS crisis, as its death toll kept hitting new peaks, the focus on the physical became manic. A community whose most public faces had been sick and dying for more than a decade seemed bent on projecting health. Fitness. Power.

Or maybe broad shoulders and abs are the mutually agreed-upon hottest things, the way blond hair and big tits are the all-access pass to the straight male world, and having them is the surest way to get yourself laid. A little of both, probably.

To be honest though, in retrospect I feel lucky that I didn't fit in, because if I had I'd have been the worst of them all. If my thick, protective layer of blubber kept some people out, it's okay, because they ended up being the right people.

The rest of the Chelsea bars followed the same template as Splash. Same guys. Same rules. Same Robin S. But I was an eager young man fresh out of Catholic school, so I kept searching. In any major city, there are gay bar magazines, tour books to the scene to tell you where to go and which nights to go there. There were two in New York at the time: *Homo Xtra* and *Next*. I grabbed them both from Splash, took them home and went at them with the Hi-Liters I'd stolen from work. My home on Upper East Side, the place where all postcollegiate prepsters settle when they move to New York, boasted affordable rents and numerous draft beer specials, but almost no gay bars. The magazines listed one ritzy piano bar in the East Sixties for guys in their seventies, another place near Bloomingdale's exclusively for Asian twinks and Asian twink enthusiasts.

And then one place called The Regent, which was summarized thusly: "A young entrepreneurial crowd mixes with an appreciative older audience." Young? *I am that!* Entrepreneurial? *I am in the world of business, sort of!* Older people? *I have been taught to respect my elders, plus think of the stories they could tell!* Sold. I dressed in my finest polo shirt and khakis and hopped on the southbound 6 train, toward my destiny.

The Regent was down by the tram to Roosevelt Island, a hidden little place without so much as a sign—just a red light over the door. *The appreciative older audience likes to relive the bad old days,* I figured. I swung open the door and entered just as "Show Me Love" by Robin S. made its crescendo. The lights were dim. The crowd was segregated: young'uns along the wall, older guys—and we are talking *older* guys— along the bar. Three empty, silent feet in between. The two groups surveyed one another. It was like a junior high mixer. I struck up a conversation with a good-looking younger guy in a very tight tank top and a goatee. "You new?" he asked, looking over my shoulder at the older gentlemen. "I am!" I said. "Well, you know. *Good luck.*" Talking did not seem to be on anyone's agenda at this place. A guy at the bar signaled him over and he went. They spoke for a quick moment, the older guy settled his tab, and they left. I stood alone, with my back against the wall, nursing a Bud Light bottle. *A cold room. It'll warm up,* I figured.

After twenty minutes or so, the drunkest of the older guys at the bar waved me over. I stepped to him.

"Hi! I'm Dave."

"You're new."

"I am!"

He looked me up and down and then up again and then down again. "How much?"

Have you ever had the experience of being in your kitchen and you see an ant, and you think "How strange, an ant," and then your scope of vision immediately widens out, and suddenly you see a *vast network of ants* who have just been there—making orderly lines, serving their queen, eating your food since God knows when—and until this moment you were utterly, blissfully blind to what was right in front of you? This was that kind of deal. Immediately I realized what any halfway-savvy fifth-grader with decent reading comprehension skills would have picked up on immediately: "young entrepreneurial types and an appreciative older audience" meant "prostitutes and johns." This was a hustler bar. I shook the hand of my appreciative older audience, finished my beer in one large gulp, and excused myself.

*   *   *

I had a hard time finding my place in New York's gay scene, and while today I recognize the problem as internalized homophobia and a lamentable eagerness to find fulfillment in a bar, at the time I blamed CeCe Peniston. Where now I recognize that the mid-'90s were a golden age of gay-bar music—a perfect, shining moment in time that has earned its place alongside the Motown era and the classic rock of the '70s—at the time it worked my nerves. But that shit holds up; go into the most basic gay bar in your area—the one that smells like an old fog machine and is called Rumors or Illusions or The Malebox or whatever—and see how long it takes for you to hear "Finally." If you have not heard it in thirty minutes or less, drinks are on me. (Limit 1, well and draft only.) In the '90s, disco was becoming less of a dirty word and the gay community was becoming a marketing segment. Suddenly all you needed was a drum machine, some rudimentary recording equipment, and a shouting black woman, and you could be a gay bar superstar. Black Box, La Bouche, Corina, Real McCoy, too many to mention. They aimed for "Let the Music Play," and when they missed, at least they landed among the "Gonna Make You Sweat"s.

There were a handful of bars in the still-intimidating East Village, and I thought if I didn't find my home there, maybe I'd just get stabbed to death and the whole thing would be less of an issue. I immediately felt more at home in these places: The Boiler Room, The Phoenix, Wonder Bar. They had less hostile guys and more adventurous ninety-nine-compact disc jukeboxes, stocked with ninety-eight fresh, interesting albums—Stereolab, Jon Spencer Blues Explosion, Soul Coughing—and, in position ninety-nine, Madonna's *Immaculate Collection*. And come 11 p.m. on a Friday night, the Chelsea boys in their Caesar haircuts would start to arrive, and your Morphine would be cut with "La Isla Bonita." It never failed.

And I never failed to show up. Up on the Upper East Side, my signature move became The Ghost. I'd be out with my friends, listening to the Dave Matthews Band at Dorrian's or The Gaf, and then, at around 2:00 a.m., after the appropriate number of draft beers, I would act very tired. Ostentatious yawns and stretches. I might tell a friend I was going home to hit the sack, or I might just leave. Either way, I'd hit the street, shake off the fake fatigue, hop in a taxi, and go downtown.

Two a.m. is the hour when people get less picky about who they talk to and possibly take home. Two a.m. is when a guy like me can shine.

When you're very young and you don't know how to find (or be) a real boyfriend yet, you make one up out of what's around. You have your friends, who take care of your emotional needs, and then you hook up with strangers, which checks off the intimacy box. You cobble satisfaction together. It's not perfect, but it works. It did for me, anyway.

The great thing about New York, I quickly learned out of necessity, is that you don't need to be in a gay bar to meet other gay people. It is a big, diverse city full of single twenty-three-year-olds who are desperate to pair themselves and their friends off so they can have dinner parties and pretend to be older than they are. There are all kinds of people, everywhere, and they are free to mix wherever they choose.

One major pitfall about being a single gay man in New York in 1994, as the community was starting to gain visibility and power, was that people—primarily women—were beginning to see gay friends as a hot accessory. They would get very familiar with you very quickly. They would tell you about their sex lives when you didn't ask. They would call you *girlfriend*. They would look at you, like a dog awaiting a treat, expecting you to say something saucy and fabulous. It's really easy to let people down in this context.

It is also very easy to *be* let down in this context. You would be set up on blind dates by people. "You have to meet my friend Thomas/Richard/Harold, you guys will be *perfect* together," someone would tell you, and then you'd go have a drink with someone with whom you have no chemistry whatsoever and realize: The reason this person thought we'd be perfect together is that we're both homosexuals and there are no other reasons. What you thought was careful matchmaking was just your friend congratulating himself for knowing two gay dudes.

Otherwise, I met and dated four kinds of guys:

- THE GUY WHO HAD JUST FIGURED OUT HE WAS GAY. Once I learned my way around the bars and clubs of the city, I found that guys like this gravitated toward me. Solid, broad-shouldered guys with names like Rob and Pete and Jim. They were not yet out of the closet, barely able to acknowledge their sexuality to themselves. So when they met me, they felt relaxed. Easy. I reminded them of their fraternity brothers. I was a guy they could drink beer and have very shallow conversations about sports with. These guys needed me. I made them feel safe. I could relate to them the way they had been taught guys should relate to one another, and then once we had drunk enough to feel comfortable with our sexual needs, they would kiss me. They would kiss with such eagerness! Such hunger and passion! We would have clumsy drunken groping sessions that we called sex, and then in two weeks they'd get tired of me and go deeper into Chelsea. I'd run into them a couple months later and they'd be in a tight tank top and a Caesar and their names would be Robert and Peter and James. I was their Ellis Island. I stamped their papers and pushed them off to a new life in a brave new land. It was sad and lonely, but somehow better than nothing.

- THE GUY WHO DEFINED HIMSELF FULLY BY BEING GAY. This guy snapped. This guy knew the Peniston deep cuts.

This guy would say things like "Andrew Shue? Oh, she's *fine*." This guy would live in the gay neighborhood and go to the gay gym and buy his gay food at the gay grocery store. This guy would say, "You live on the Upper East Side? Girl, *why?*" This guy couldn't see a life outside of the gay bubble and didn't want to. And if I would express interest in doing something else, not even something *straight*, just something *else*, the response would be some variant of: "You want to see *Pulp Fiction?* Girl, you are so self-loathing." They were right, of course, but I had much better and more sophisticated reasons for hating myself than just for liking boys.

- THE GUY WHO DEFINED HIMSELF FULLY BY BEING UN-GAY. This guy burped. This guy knew the Hootie deep cuts. This guy would say things like "Who's Andrew Shue? Oh, he's on *Melrose Place?* That's for fags." This guy would live anywhere but Chelsea and would be out of the closet, but would be so desperate to convince you he wasn't one of *those* kinds of guys that it would immediately be exhausting. It's the flip side of the coin, but it's the same shitty coin.

- MESSES. And then there were the drunk-on-Saturday-afternoon, sexually compulsive, emotionally stunted and volatile messes who couldn't connect with another human being if their life depended on it, which it pretty much did.

I also *was* all four of these guys. And I get it; we had all, in our own time and in our own ways, come to the realization that we were a part of a segment of the population that we'd been told all our lives was bad. Broken. Embarrassing. Un-healthy. Those words applied to *us* now, and we had to figure out what we were going to do with them.

And because we were trying to be men, we mostly did it alone.

The Men Who Ruined Me

SO LISTEN: I have no idea how sexual orientation is determined, and I don't really care. Some say it's genetic, which the Tony Perkinses of the world refute because no specific evidence of a gay gene has been found, and as we all know, everything that hasn't been discovered yet doesn't exist. (It's why we canceled science and told all the researchers to go home.) Others say it's environmental, and point to the fact that the more older brothers a boy has, the higher his chances of being gay, which makes me feel even worse for those younger Duggars. I would imagine it's a combination of the two, plus, in my case, a megadose of scorching hot men in the popular culture of my adolescence. I'm not saying these guys made me gay, though they probably did; what I am saying is that they cast a shadow that stretched all the way into my adulthood. Here are a few of the men whose impact on my young psyche made it impossible for me to commit to any actual human beings I met in later life.

Huey Lewis

The first ten seconds of the video for "I Want A New Drug" rearranged me at the cellular level in ways that I am only now able to understand. They are elegant in their simplicity: a hungover Huey Lewis wakes up and putters around his San Francisco apartment, in boxer shorts. That's it. He is just a grown man with a thick outgrowth of chest hair in a sensible pair of boxers in America's gay-friendliest city. He fills a sink with ice and water and dunks his head in, because this is a man who understands self-care. He is just the tiniest bit depraved, and he knows how to bring himself back to life for showtime. He can pull off a red suit. He does not try to be sexy, and he is therefore the sexiest thing going. He even gets a little come-hither stare from a guy on the ferry to Sausalito, and takes it in stride. The man is a magician, and I would still hit it, just tell me where to be.

Nicolas Cage in *Valley Girl*

This one has gone entirely off the rails in the last decade or so, to the degree that from today's perspective it's actually startling how hot he was in his youth. But good Lord, he is something in *Valley Girl*. Soulful basset-hound eyes, chest hair in a perfect Superman-logo pattern, the very best of Merry Go Round's 1983 men's collection, great taste in music. He's from the wrong side of the Hollywood Hills, and we don't even hear about his parents, much less meet them, like we do her health-food-store-owning folks. He doesn't wear the right clothes, he has a jazzy streak of red through his hair, he has a goofy best friend who wears equally mall-punky clothes and their relationship is either kind of homoerotic or I just remember it that way because I wanted to see them kiss. Either way, I credit him with getting me into two important things: The Plimsouls and dudes.

Ted McGinley

Before he was on *Married With Children*, I knew Ted McGinley as The Hot Guy Who Showed Up Places. Oh, there's Ted in short shorts on *The Love Boat* as jocky Ship Photographer Ace, the year the boat had a full-time dance team on it. Hello, here's Ted in running shorts in *Revenge of the Nerds* as the president of the evil jock fraternity. Whoomp, there he is on *Happy Days* as . . . I don't remember, but some kind of jock, probably. If a script called for an obscenely handsome guy with a tasteful tan and perfect legs, the casting director called Ted McGinley, and two to five percent of America's preteen boys took special notice.

Everyone in the Volleyball Scene in *Top Gun*

I mean, *Top Gun* is deeply homoerotic, full stop; it's Tom Cruise in the Navy, for Pete's sake. But by the time Maverick, Goose, Iceman, and Slider took to the sandpit for the volleyball game, it was all over. A young Tom Cruise who is somehow all trapezius muscle. A Val Kilmer in full bloom. An Anthony Edwards, who takes a good long look at his costars and wisely keeps his shirt on. And then there's Rick Rossovich, whose body is an absolute marvel of engineering, and who, in the middle of everything—as a fey Kenny Loggins song called "Playing with the Boys" hits the nail right on the head—strikes a bodybuilding pose. Dude somehow flexes every single muscle from his waist to the ends of his hair, as though this were a thing people did in the middle of beach volleyball games (which I am sorry to tell you it is not). In this moment, anyone who may have been on the fence about their sexuality simply surrendered. Gayness had us on target lock.

Jake Ryan in *Sixteen Candles*

Here's how hot Jake Ryan in *Sixteen Candles* is: all we know about him is that he sits idly by while his girlfriend throws a party that destroys his parents' house; he spends the whole thing up in his bedroom trying to call a girl two years younger than him in the middle of the night; he's a little bit racist to Long Duk Dong (which, in fairness, so is John Hughes) and he sends his blackout-drunk girlfriend home with a boy who doesn't have a driver's license, with the clear understanding that this boy is going to at least try to have sexual intercourse with her. And yet every time I watch the movie, I am left thinking: "That's the guy for me." That is a powerful thing right there. That is weaponized hotness. No wonder the actor who played him left the business and moved to rural Pennsylvania to make furniture; the responsibility must have been too great. (Unfortunately for him, the idea of a Jake Ryan who rejected the industry and makes armoires in a forest with his hands is about the hottest thing I can imagine.)

Herb Tarlek in *WKRP in Cincinnati*

Beats me, folks. I just know it's true.

Wearers of the High-Waisted Jeans of the 1980s to Early 1990s

There was a time when men's jeans actually told you what was going on in the crotch and buttock area of the American male. Things got kind of packagey. You could tell a soccer guy from a hockey guy if you spent enough time staring and analyzing. Back in the day, a pair of jeans straight-up announced a butt. Now, who even knows what's happening down there? Sure, we have banished acid-wash back to Hell, but at what cost? Hurry up and cycle back around, fashion.

David Lee Roth

Another questionable one, but the crotch wants what it wants. He is loose-limbed, flexible, hairy-chested, always up for a good time; his hair has body and volume. A friend of mine saw his comeback tour a couple of years ago, and I asked how old David Lee looked, and he said: "Like a creature from Hebrew mythology." But we'll always have the cover of *Crazy from the Heat.*

10

The Man Who Sold the World

IN THE MID-'90S, SAATCHI & SAATCHI WAS AN ADVERtising agency right out of an '80s romantic comedy. The halls were filled with attractive and witty young people in stylish clothing. Each floor had a playroom with pinball machines and Nintendo and Pop-A-Shot, so that when you needed to take a break and refill the tank, you could go engage with your inner child. We took part in agency-wide brainstorming sessions, where no matter your position or department, you could weigh in on the new Fruit Roll-Up/Go-Gurt Squeezer crossover product. There were kegs in the atrium on Friday evenings and no such thing as "Friday evenings" until after Labor Day, because in the summertime you broke the hell out at 1:00 p.m., so the people who could afford it could make the Hampton Jitney.

And if I didn't know exactly what I was doing—and I didn't have one goddamn clue—it didn't exactly matter. The advertising industry runs on a certain amount of witty fecklessness, on charm, on talk. As an executive, you need to be fast enough on your feet to change a pitch halfway through if you sense that the client isn't feeling it, and you have to learn that agility somewhere. I learned it by being careless and making clerical errors both large and small nearly every day. *"What's that?*

This entire spreadsheet is based on the wrong budget numbers? My bad. Where'd you get those shoes?" If you can make people like you, your incompetence can come to be seen as a sweet little peccadillo. In this regard, I brought exactly the right skill set to the table.

Each year, Saatchi would hire a new crop of young recruits right out of college. The ones from Dartmouth and Brown would go right into the account management department, where they'd learn to be the liaisons between the creatives and the clients. The ones from the sub-Ivies would go into media planning, where we'd place the actual advertisements in magazines, on billboards, on prime-time television. My teammates were Scott, a handsome hockey player from Quinnipiac; Kathryn, a preppy young go-getter from Colgate; and Janet, a dramatic young woman from Sarah Lawrence. Out at lunch together on our first day at Toukie's, a restaurant on Hudson Street owned by Robert De Niro's girlfriend and season-five *227* star Toukie Smith, we got to know each other. Scott was into baseball and Soundgarden; Kathryn wanted to start her own agency someday; Janet liked *Beverly Hills, 90210.* No, but Janet *really* liked *Beverly Hills, 90210.* Her cubicle was like a high school locker plastered with pictures of Luke Perry, Jason Priestley, and Gabrielle Carteris. It was unseemly, but then I had a poster for *Threesome,* the Josh Charles/Lara Flynn Boyle/Stephen Baldwin bi-curiosity vehicle, pinned up over my Compaq desktop in a clumsy, coming half-out maneuver, so I had no room to talk.

The advertising business, like all business, was flush in 1994. Brands, agencies and media outlets had more money than they know how to spend, but they displayed a real eagerness to learn. Mostly, this meant parties. Pretty much every weeknight, a different magazine would throw itself a bash to celebrate its new editorial direction, milestone issue, or youth-targeted offshoot. High-ceilinged spaces in the Meatpacking District or SoHo were festooned with banners saluting *Cosmopolitan*'s "Fun Fearless Female" initiative or the debut issue of Time Inc.'s *InStyle*. There would be a twenty-minute performance from Del Amitri or Da Brat. There would be a signature cocktail whose primary ingredient was the party's co-sponsor, which would require you to quickly acquire a taste for Alizé or Zima Gold. There were trays of hors d'oeuvres, which would invariably become our dinner, because on an entry-level advertising salary, one must choose between groceries and a social life, and the latter will always win. On the way out, you would get a gift bag with a compilation CD of Sony artists and some sample-size facial scrubs. It was an Olsen Twins TV adaptation of a Jay McInerney book.

These events were full of twenty-six-year-olds on the make, and as they seemed intimidatingly old and sophisticated, I mostly hung with Janet and talked *90210*. I got the full scoop on how she thought the gang was adjusting to life at California University, what she thought of Steve's involvement with the KEG house, and ultimately whether Mark David Espinoza's Jesse was really what Andrea needed in a partner. Janet really went there, *90210*-wise. She had theories and opinions, and she would back that shit up with facts and figures. "Dave, I think you're way off the mark when you talk about Donna's behavior at the prom. You *know* how she was raised and what's in her bloodline." One night I met Janet's roommate Jennifer at an event for *Country Living* magazine—held at Kelley

& Ping's Chinese restaurant on Sullivan Street, sponsored by Jack Daniels and Kraft's new Lem'N Berry Sippers lemonade powders—and said, "So Janet really likes *90210*, huh?"

She said, "Oh, you have no idea."

I said, "Please give me an idea."

"Well, on Wednesday nights at nine o'clock, she will call her father, and they'll discuss the issues that were raised in the episode they've just watched."

"Even in the summer?"

"Even in reruns. They'll catch new things on the second watch."

I asked, "Is there any way I can come by and eavesdrop on one of these conversations?"

She said, "I think I have an opening in five weeks."

That summer, Fox announced that Shannen Doherty would not be returning to the cast of *Beverly Hills, 90210*, and I got the news, as we all did, via the purple section of *USA Today*. The revelation came completely out of the blue, because there was no such thing as an entertainment-gossip website, only your own gut to tell you what a pain in the ass Shannen Doherty was to work with. Scott came to my desk, then Kathryn. We all had one thing on our minds, and we didn't even have to say it out loud: Who's going to tell Janet? We decided it would be best if we were all there, because we were a family of a sort, and also because nobody wanted to miss her reaction. I brought the Life section with me as we visited Janet's cubicle, sensing that she would need to see it in writing, but when we got there it was clear that her father had already called. She was crying. She took a personal day. It was for the best. And although the news ruined her month and she would leave meetings right in the middle because she was too upset to go on, I respected her passion.

Saatchi's goal was to shape us all up into well-rounded young advertising people. For the first year, we'd all be moved around from department to department, spending a few weeks with the gang at Kids' Cereals, a month or so at Sauza Tequila and Little Caesar's. At the end of the year, one of the places we'd visited would claim us, and that's where we'd work. It was a company-wide fraternity rush. Our jobs were purely administrative: we'd type up presentations, make charts, and distribute memos, which we had to do by hand because there was no such thing as e-mail yet. (The future reached us in early 1995, but it was only an interoffice e-mail program and you couldn't attach documents, so if you wanted someone to look at a spreadsheet, you had to print it out onto paper and put it in front of their face like some kind of lackey in a historical drama.) And because we were recent college graduates, we were doing these jobs on a maximum of three hours of sleep, cheap draft beer emanating from every pore.

In October, I was working in the sports media department with the guys—and they were all *guys*—who placed the Citizen watch ads around the court in the US Open and the beer ads in NFL games. Personality-wise, I got along with my bosses beautifully, and if the department's specialty bumped up the difficulty setting of a job I was already struggling to understand, at least I was picking up a new skill, which was pretending to talk about sports. (Here's my strategy: I would look for an opportunity to say "Where was the D?" and then create a distraction.)

A couple Fridays into my tenure as a sports media guy, my

boss Bob swung by my desk. Bob told me that his boss, Mike, and Rick, the guy whose position I was currently filling, had won last year's annual Inter-Agency 3-on-3 Basketball Tournament in a squeaker over Young & Rubicam. Now that Rick was at another agency, they were down a man. "Oh, no," I said, and before I had an opportunity to ask him where the D was, he said, "It starts next Thursday. Do you play?"

I did not play. I had never played. I did not want to play. But I was desperate to please my new superiors, I was learning new things about myself every day, and I was still very much holding on to the feeling that sports were a thing I was supposed to do. So I said yes. Yes, I will play basketball for the first time in my life in front of my new bosses and co-workers and any number of people in my industry at New York City's annual Inter-Agency 3-on-3 Basketball Tournament. This was going to be great.

The reality of my situation set in before the scent of Bob's CK One left my cubicle. I had six days to learn everything there is to know about basketball, up to and beyond how the scoring works. I called my college friend Chris, whom I had seen play and decided was therefore an expert, and explained my predicament. "Could we," I asked, "have a little crash course over the weekend?" He laughed and agreed. And then he kept laughing, and I hung up.

Saturday morning came, and Chris met me at the courts in Gracie Park. "Okay, Dave," he said. "Show me what you got." He chest-passed me the ball, and I caught it, which was honestly a bit of a surprise even though he was three feet away. I ran around the court a little bit, and I shot in the direction of the basket a few times. I actually got it onto the backboard once, and my level of confidence shot up a couple of notches.

I started running faster, shifting my weight foot-to-foot, pivoting like I'd seen people do. Running. Feeling strong, free. Feeling more and more like the baller I had secretly always been. I took another shot. I made it. I had *game*. I looked at Chris, raised my eyebrows, and chest-passed the ball back to him. *How ya like me now?* my face said.

"Okay, that was good. One thing, though: in basketball, when you're moving, you have to *dribble the ball*," he said, maintaining eye contact and nodding as he spoke, the way you do when you're giving directions to foreigners. "You have to dribble it all of the time." Shit. I *knew that*.

Chris showed me some of the basics, and then saw in my face what "the basics" were going to mean in this context, and then showed me *those* basics. Slowly, we started to actually play. I felt myself getting stronger, less self-conscious. Chris was patient, and I was an eager learner. I felt as though I was living a sports-movie training montage in real time. We went on this way for a good hour or so, until we were both sweating and panting. We were *playing basketball*. We were *doing this*. And then Chris put his hand on my shoulder, gave it a good squeeze, and looked me in the eye, saying, "Dave, you have to stop this basketball tournament from happening."

We agreed that I would borrow an ankle splint and crutches that Chris had around from an old injury, and that I would hobble into work on Monday and tell them the bad news. Which I did. So they asked another dude in the kids' cereals department, who said yes, and they won the whole thing again. Their D was on point, probably.

After the decline of my basketball career, I continued to work my way through the whole agency in my fraternity rush year, hoping to find a match. While I made a lot of friends and went to a lot of parties, I didn't really fit anywhere, due in large part to my incompetence vastly outweighing my charm. A few months later, I got a call from a headhunter who was trying to fill an opening at Grey in Midtown. It was for a junior account-executive position on a Procter & Gamble account. A move up. A rise in pay. I put in a résumé, got an interview, and then got myself an offer. I accepted, because although I had already bitten off more than I could chew, I didn't know that you're allowed to stop biting.

I said goodbye to whimsical, candy-colored Saatchi and went to serious, gray Grey, where my first job was to put together a deck for a mid-year presentation to the client, Cover Girl. It was a straightforward job.

I fucked it up so badly I was fired for gross incompetence within three weeks.

You know the Peter Principle? The notion that people get promoted throughout their careers until they get to the job they cannot do? I got to that point at age twenty-three.

I temped for a few months, then landed on my feet by the grace of my mouth and got myself another, simpler gig at another agency uptown, where I still wasn't very good, but would do.

The experience left a mark, though. The universe was sending me a message. I wanted to try something new. I wanted to find my place in the world. I wanted to be as openly passionate as Janet was about the Walsh family, and get paid for it.

I wanted to be . . . I don't know, *something*.

11

Impulsive

I HAVE NEVER BEEN A DRUGS GUY, BECAUSE NANCY REAgan did her job well. "Just Say No" was a ridiculously simplistic response to the multi-layered problem of drug abuse and organized crime in the United States, but that shit worked on a lot of us '80s teenagers. Nancy Reagan was America's Postwar Mom for a minute there—which is to say withholding and emotionally remote—and we didn't want to let her down. Plus the message was so simple: Just say no! Don't be bad, be good instead! Easy, practical, effective.

It worked on me.

Except for two times.

On a Saturday night in the winter of 1992, when I was a sophomore in college, I was preparing for a night out when my friend Andrew pulled me aside and asked, "Do you want to do Ecstasy?" Ecstasy was a brand-new thing in those days, and Holy Cross was not a drugsy campus, but somehow I had presented myself as a person who was up for anything. I threw caution, good sense, and Nancy Reagan out the window.

"Sure."

Andrew had come by two hits of E at $25 piece from a friend at a more adventurous college while he was home for the Christmas break, and he had never done it before either.

He brought them back to the Cross, waiting for the perfect opportunity and the perfect person to do it with, which apparently were *right now* and *me*. His roommate was gone for the weekend, so we went back to his room, two dorms down from my own. He put *Achtung Baby* on the CD player, and pulled a Ziploc bag out from the back of his T-shirt drawer. The pills were massive, like something you'd give horses. Each was the exact size and color of an orange Chewy SweeTart. We broke them up with our keys and gobbled up the pieces.

A few minutes later, Andrew's phone rang. It was his girlfriend, who lived off-campus. Andrew said, "Uh-huh. Uh-huh. Okay. See you." He hung up, looked at me, and said, "She wants me to come over. Make yourself at home here if you want. Have a good night."

And then he left.

And as The Edge's majestic guitar introduced "Who's Gonna Ride Your Wild Horses," my situation became clear to me. I was alone in a room that was not my own, in a hall where I did not live, waiting for a drug I had never taken—and could not tell anyone I had taken, for fear of getting a reputation—to kick in. Would it happen in a minute? An hour? Five hours? Andrew wouldn't have had the answers even if he hadn't left, which he had. I was in the single-rider line for what could either be a brief, gentle whirl in the teacups or a Space Mountain that would never stop for the rest of my life.

The thing about E is that it kicks in all at once. Your entire body begins to tingle, but not in a pleasant, love-struck way. It's more like your foot is asleep, but everywhere. Your heart rate leaps like you've gotten a massive electrical shock. It is an instant panic attack, particularly if you are doing it in total isolation and "Mysterious Ways" is thumping out of a boom box that is not your own. I would have put a finger on my wrist to take my pulse, but I could actually see my veins and arteries pump pump pumping through my skin. Much too fast. *Deep breaths, Dave.* I grabbed Andrew's phone and cradled it in my arms like a fragile newborn baby whose umbilical cord was gray, ten feet long, and stuck into the wall. I told myself I'd call 911 if it got even one percent scarier. Oh, but then an ambulance would come and people would talk. No good.

I was going to have to get myself out of this situation. I was going to need a plan. I got up and started pacing, telephone in my sweaty hands.

Boxy, affordable sportcoats from places like The Gap and Structure were popular that year, and I wore them often. I enjoyed the slight Thurston Howell air they lent me, plus there were pockets the perfect size for cigarettes and a Walkman. I fished around for a Camel Light to calm me down. But instead, in my breast pocket, there was something smaller and harder than a pack of cigarettes.

Something *perfect.*

In the left breast pocket of my black watch plaid sportcoat was a cassette copy of the self-titled debut album by Wilson Phillips.

I pulled it out of its case, and stuck it into Andrew's boom box with shaking, addled hands. I rewound it to the beginning, hit play, and walked over to Andrew's full-length mirror to take a good look at myself.

And then track one kicked in.

You will recall that track one is leadoff single "Hold On."

"I know there's pain," Chynna Phillips told me. You know it, sister. It hit me in this moment that I had a clear choice between joy and fear, between anxiety and actual literal ecstasy, that if I was choosing to freak out, I could just as easily choose not to. Why *do* I lock myself up in these chains? *Is* it really fair to feel this way inside?

I spoke out loud to my reflection: "You hold on, Dave Holmes. Things will change. Things will go your way."

The clouds parted, and a feeling like a combination of strong coffee, an orgasm, and the first warm day of spring trickled into my body. My blood was carbonated. This was *great*. And as Wilson Phillips predicted, something did make me want to turn around and say goodbye. Goodbye to the isolation, to the fear, to anything that held me back. I threw open the door to Andrew's room, just as people began their Keystone Light–fueled pre-gaming for a Saturday night. I went room to room, delivering tight hugs and kind words, because even if I wasn't real familiar with the kids on this hall, I knew they were the finest people I would ever meet. We had a connection. Every song on everyone's stereo was the best song I had ever heard, until I got sick of it about twenty seconds in, and then *would you mind if I changed it?*

Life was beautiful. This was the way a person was supposed to feel.

That was the night Nirvana—*they're my new favorite group, can I tell you about them?*—made their *Saturday Night Live* debut. I had a viewing party in Andrew's room. It was also the first night of the Beth Cahill/Melanie Hutsell/Siobhan Fallon era of *SNL*, and when the three ladies came out for their Delta Delta Delta sketch? I don't need to tell you that I had never seen a funnier, truer thing.

That nobody around me thought anything more than "Dave Holmes is in a moderately good mood" speaks either to how sheltered we were at Holy Cross, or to how much pressure

I put on myself to behave like a person on Ecstasy at all times just to be accepted. Probably both.

It was a great night. But here's the thing I learned about E: let's say we're only eligible to receive a finite amount of happiness units for any given day. Let's say ten happiness units. Usually you get six to eight, sometimes you only get two, once in a very rare while you get all ten.

Ecstasy gives you fifty happiness units, all at the same time. And it feels great to have five days' full happiness allowance all at the same time! You don't know what to do with it all, where to put it, who to give it to. You're lousy with happiness units!

But then the next day, and the few days after, you do not have any happiness units at all, because you've used them all up in one go. You have to learn how to live for a few days with zero happiness units, and no eligibility to apply for more. It is literally physically impossible for you to get happy. You do things like turn on the radio, hear "The Way It Is" by Tesla, and openly sob. (Which I did the very next morning. The line "That's the way it is, the way that it goes" was too real for me.)

So I know two things for sure: one, Ecstasy was a one-and-done for me, and two, I would have been the one person who ended up in a mental institution from a single dose of Ecstasy if it had not been for Wilson Phillips.

So that was it for me and drugs. It would be one tiny indiscretion, I told myself. Nancy need never know.

Except for this one other thing, which happened in 1996, after I got canned from Grey. I was sighing, roaming the streets of Manhattan dejected and in tweed. I was temping as a typist for Credit Suisse First Boston, taking gruff orders from financial analysts who were my age. The agency that assigned me there was called Mademoiselle, and when I checked in at security, I had to give the name of the agency and then my own, which meant I had to start each work day by saying, "Mademoiselle Dave Holmes." I was at an emotional low. Ripe for the picking.

I had just begun doing some short-form improv shows at various bars around town—bars that had stages, but whose regulars never showed up expecting to see a show. We'd do our little games: World's Worst (where you go off audience suggestions and act like the world's worst porn star or prostitute or . . . really those are the only two suggestions you'll ever get), ABC Shakespeare (where you improvise a Shakespeare scene except the first line starts with A and the next line starts with B, and then someone says "Zounds" at the end because it's Shakespeare-y sounding and nothing else starts with Z), the thing where you put your arms behind your back and someone puts their arms through yours so it's like their arms are your arms, and you have to justify what they're doing. All the hits. And we did it all for the backs of people's heads as they watched the game, or for small groups of Danish travelers who saw this bar in their travel guide. It was demoralizing, but we were doing it together. Comedy boot camp.

One night I had a really good show, which is to say someone turned around to face us, or understood our language, or seemed to laugh when I said "Zounds." When you're just starting out in comedy, that's all it takes to make you feel like you've found your calling. I thought: *I am strong, I am invincible, I am comedy.* I had some post-show drinks at the bar with my teammates and headed for home. It was a Thursday and I had work in the morning.

When I got back to my building, there were voices coming from my neighbor Adam's place. Adam was one of those Wall

Street types who ran in a more glamorous social circle, but we had become drinks-every-couple-of-months kind of friends. I heard whooping and laughter as I turned my key. It seemed like he and his banker boys were having fun in there. I was the future of American comedy. I deserved to have fun with cool people. I was also a little tipsy. I knocked.

It turned out that Adam had a gang of college friends in town for a fraternity brother's bachelor party out on Long Island. He'd taken the next day off of work, and he and his handsome, white-toothed posse were gathered around his Crate & Barrel coffee table doing cocaine off a Pharcyde CD cover.

I had always said that I would never do cocaine, but that was before what may or may not have been a laugh from a stranger had kick-started my next life. I was a new man now, and that man was impervious to consequences. Plus, I had instant crushes on about four of these six guys.

"You want in?" one of them asked, handing me a short straw and *Bizarre Ryde II Tha Pharcyde*.

"You know what? I *do* want in." I put the straw in my nose, leaned forward, inhaled a line, and nothing happened.

And then four seconds later I was the happiest, warmest, and most confident I'd ever been, and the next thing I knew I was in an all-night jazz club in the West Village.

Loving it.

Loving my new friends and my new favorite kind of music and my new frame of mind and my new life.

I love this! I get this! I get jazz and I love jazz! I get why everyone is kind of looking at the musicians and nodding knowingly! I am nodding myself! Actually all of my limbs are moving! I am a jazz and cocaine person! Let's talk about jazz! Do you like jazz? Who is your favorite jazz person? That guy playing jazz up there on stage right now? That's so funny because he's mine too! Let's celebrate by doingmorecocainerightnow.

Aside from the fact that it makes you think and speak in italics, here is the thing I learned very quickly about cocaine: it is always *almost* the most fun you have ever had. On a scale of zero to ten, zero being your life before you discovered cocaine, and ten being the best time you have ever had in your entire life, better than Ecstasy, better than Space Mountain even, cocaine puts you at a 9.8. But cocaine also makes you greedy. A 9.8 just *will not do*. You can see a perfect ten from where you are sitting (and fidgeting and chewing the inside of your cheek). That ten is right there. You want it. And the only thing you can think of that will get you to a ten is more cocaine.

You decide that it is a perfectly healthy decision for you to reorient your life fully around cocaine. So you keep doing more, every ten minutes or so, chasing a kind of bliss that does not exist, until there is no more cocaine to do, and you have to face what you have become, which is a toilet person.

For me and my new best friends, that time came at around 10:00 the next morning, long after I had called in sick to my temp agency from a West Village payphone at 5:00 a.m. We sat in my living room with the TV on, scraping up whatever trace amounts existed on my coffee table, which is to say aspirating dust mites while Rosie O'Donnell fired Koosh balls into her audience and called people "cutie patooties."

When there is no more cocaine to do, the crash begins, and there is nothing you can do about it. The quickened heart rate that was exhilarating only moments before is now cause for alarm. The perspiration that gave you a sexy glow under jazz-club neon makes you look like a sweaty fat person in the morning sun. The head that was a Tesla coil of brilliant ideas at midnight is a half-deflated basketball at dawn.

It is awful.

When I am feeling low, I know I can always do one of two things to turn my mood around: I can take a nap, or I can masturbate. In particularly dark times, I find that I can bounce back and forth between the two, all day long. Cocaine will rob you of these two valuable tools. Once I finally decided to call it a night at around noon, I found myself sweating through my sheets, fitfully trying to engage a dick that wanted nothing to do with me. My only option was to stare at the ceiling and pray for my heart rate to return to normal. It was a physical hangover unlike nothing I had ever felt, but the mental and spiritual aspects were far worse. The self-loathing descended and carried me off like the Wicked Witch's flying monkeys. *Look at what you've become, Dave Holmes. You weren't ever going to do cocaine, and now you have. You're damaged goods. You're a druggie. You're one of those girls who tried to get Punky Brewster to join their gang. You're what Nancy Reagan warned you about.*

You're disgusting.

And last night's show was mediocre at best.

Obviously, the only way to silence these voices was to do more cocaine. I had asked Adam for his dealer's number—the guy's name, I swear to God, was Rocko—and I fumbled for my jeans and fished it out of the front pocket. I remembered Adam telling me that a gram cost $40. I went to the Chase Bank ATM at the corner of Eighty-sixth and Lexington.

I had $32. My direct deposit wouldn't reflect my latest paycheck until midnight.

I got saved from a terrible decision that would have altered the course of my life irrevocably, by a slight bank delay. If I had had $8 more, I would probably be dead right now.

Months later, those same boys came back to town for that fraternity brother's wedding. I told Adam I'd be around that weekend in case we wanted to get the gang back together— just for a beer, to reminisce. I missed them, somehow. We had bonded. We had bonded over jazz.

Adam put his hand on my shoulder and broke the news gently but firmly. "Dave, they . . . they did not care for you one bit."

I was not the future of comedy. I was not a glamorous cocaine person. I was not cool.

I was going to have to keep trying.

12

Wannabe

MTV'S FIRST *WANNA BE A VJ* AUDITION WAS AN EVENT that fundamentally changed the course of my life, and what haunts me about it now is how close I came to not going.

A few days before, I had been dicking around at my desk on a Thursday morning that was probably a busy one for whoever was doing what was supposed to be my job, when I clicked over to Billboard.com to check the charts, a weekly habit at the time. (K-Ci & JoJo had just leapt to #1 on the Hot 100 in an impressive two weeks with "All My Life," while Robbie Williams's "Let Me Entertain You" debuted at #4 on the UK charts; as ever, the Brits knew what was up.) And there, on the news feed down the right side of the screen, was the headline: MTV TO HOLD OPEN CALL FOR NEW VJ. I remember saying, in full voice: "*Hel*-lo." For months, I'd been thinking I needed to make a lateral move to some other industry. I was living in New York City, working at a job I hated, and doing it terribly; I could do that in St. Louis and live like a king. If I was going to live in the hardest, most-expensive, most-stressful city in the country, I might as well do something I liked and wasn't lousy at; it seemed a simple gift I could give myself. But I had no idea how to do that, and showing up at an open call was as good an idea as any I'd had. (If you have read this book in order, you will have noticed that my ideas were generally not very good.)

The audition was to be held at the brand-new MTV studio at 1515 Broadway, just down the road from my agency, the next Monday, April 13. I circled the date in my day planner and made a note on my PalmPilot: *call in sick.*

I tried not to imagine that I would actually pass through this audition and get anywhere. I told myself: This is a way to meet people. This is a networking opportunity. But of course, my mind went there. A lot. Like, what if they hire me and I end up on-air? Would I be friends with Duff? Would I get a muffin basket from Martha Quinn? How often does the society of current and former VJs get together? Is it a potluck kind of situation?

Sunday, April 12, was Easter, and my friends and I were too broke to spend it with our families or get a decent brunch anywhere, so we did our budget version of a Circle Line tour, also known as taking the Staten Island Ferry there and back. We celebrated the risen Christ with Budweiser tallboys and ham sandwiches. We wore pastels. We stayed up late. I didn't tell anybody what I was doing, because what I was doing was ridiculous. I was a twenty-seven-year-old man, with bills in my name and a job that people would give an arm for. I was going to stand in a line and audition to be an MTV VJ? Preposterous.

It was so stupid I had to do it.

It is important to know yourself, and what I knew about myself was that I wasn't going to blow them away with my outsized personality. I wasn't going to overwhelm them with my looks. I was a chubby, average-looking guy who could hold a conversation, and while people like that are likely to be in short supply at an open call for MTV VJs, people like that ought to arrive early, before the casting people get sick of faces and voices. For an average person to make an impression, it is important to get there before humanity becomes a giant, irritating blur. I set my alarm for 4:00 a.m.

My alarm went off at 4:00 a.m. I rolled over and looked at the giant red numerals. Blinking, screeching: 4:00. My first thought that morning was *What the fuck are you even thinking?* Perhaps this is a thing you've done yourself: you make a plan to get up and hit the gym before work, or to run around the park, or to surf as the sun is rising. At night, warm and energetic and lit from within by a few beers, it seems like exactly the right thing to do. "We'll go together," you tell your friends. "Meet you there at five." You agree. You rejoice. It's so simple to live the right way! And then your alarm goes off, and you remember that neither you nor your friends are this kind of person at all, and you reset it for your regular waking time and go back to sleep, secure in the knowledge that all of your friends have done the same thing. So it was on this morning: I stared at those numbers, my eyes burning with the desire to re-close. *Seriously, what the fuck are you even thinking, showing up to an open call like some kind of jackass. Lining up to introduce videos to a demographic you have aged out of. It's embarrassing. How dare you?*

And then one thought saved me, and one thought only: *On the other hand, you hate and are terrible at your job.*

I got up and showered.

As now, my wardrobe was very "aging prep-school boy:" lots of Brooks Brothers button-downs, lots of khakis. I put on the closest thing I had to a hip outfit: a navy sweater with one red stripe through it, blue jeans, and my one pair of John Fluevog shoes. I was as on trend as I was ever going to be.

Four-twenty a.m. is the only time when there is no traffic in New York City, so I hailed a cab with ease and made it from the Upper East Side to Forty-fourth and Broadway in less than ten minutes. The official auditions wouldn't start until 9:00, but the line wound around the building. I was #168. The 167 people who beat me there were exactly what I expected: show-biz fellas with big smiles and too-firm handshakes. Long Island girls with loud, trumpety voices and all the makeup. A couple of metal guys who agreed they should go in there and tell MTV to play some *real* shit. And just a few people ahead of me, a very tall gamine with ratted hair and a tattered army jacket covered in punk buttons. *Well, she's interesting,* I thought.

The thing about any kind of audition is that most people think the waiting room is the real proving ground. *Dazzle your fellow hopefuls with your talent and personality;* that's their motto. *Get in their heads so that when they make it into the audition room, they're feeling inadequate in the sparkle department.* The secret, I have learned, is to simply let these people tucker themselves out. Having had the foresight to bring my Discman along, I popped my headphones on and let Whiskeytown's "Strangers Almanac"—the first we would hear of a young Ryan Adams—drown out some desperate attempts at psychological warfare.

At around 8:00, some production assistants came around with forms to fill out, including a questionnaire, to which a Polaroid would be stapled. *How would your friends describe you? What's the last CD you bought? In high school, you were voted most likely to . . .* I wrote in ". . . introduce the latest Savage Garden video." I had had extensive comedy training, you guys.

Just before 9:00, they started letting people in, and once we got in front of 1515 Broadway, the line began to snake back and forth, like we were waiting for a ride at Disneyland. As the line moved, I kept passing the beautiful androgyne in the army jacket—this way, then that way, then this way. She was a foot taller than anyone else in the line, and she seemed in a very real sense to be in her own atmosphere. Her face was serene and hopeful. Or just completely blotto. It was hard to say.

At 9:15-ish, I got through the doors, up the escalator, and down the hallway full of backlit promo posters of shows (*Singled Out! The Real World! Dead At 21!*) and artists (Madonna! The Fugees! *Hanson!*). Shit was getting real.

Finally, I walked into the 1515 Broadway studio. The studio was, I would later learn, actually three studios that could be turned into one massive one, like a hotel ballroom. And if this were a movie, which in my memory it is, the camera would do a full 360-degree circle around my head before settling on my dazzled face as I took it all in. It was huge and humming with activity. Twelve audition stations ringed the room, against floor-to-ceiling windows that overlooked Times Square, a part of town I'd always done my best to avoid, but with which I was suddenly, deeply in love. Production assistants hurried to and fro, toting clipboards and following instructions their bosses gave them through their earpieces. The big wigs, who in this case were a maximum of thirty-two years old, sat along the periphery and surveyed the action. Carson Daly, handsome as on TV and somehow taller, prepared to do a VJ segment from the middle of the action, just as I might do someday. There was a palpable sense of joy in the air. The MTV gang was busy, but busy doing something they loved and were happy to do. Following their bliss, even if their bliss stressed them out a little. It was a world where people devoted all of their energy to all of the silly things I loved, and it was *right here,* eight blocks down from my office. It had been here, right under my nose, the whole time. Like Narnia.

We were called up to the audition stations twelve at a time. I went to station #5, where a guy named Joe sat me down on a stool and talked me through the process: "'Kay—we're gonna just talk for a minute, so just be natural and be yourself and don't worry about it, 'kay? And then we'll read some shit and then that'll be that, 'kay? S'gonna be fun." 'Kay. I was ready. He bent down to grab his clipboard of questions and his T-shirt rode up, revealing a tattoo of two cherries, like you'd see on a slot machine, just above his ass-crack. I loved Joe immediately. I have no idea what we talked about or what I read or how long I was there—I remember it the way one would remember a really fun car crash—but apparently Joe saw something in me. He pulled a yellow slip of paper from his clipboard, signed it, and handed it to me. "'Kay, girl— here's what you're gonna do next: you're gonna go over to the Downtown Studio and you're gonna talk to the people there, 'kay? Just ask one of those bitches with a headset how to get there. You got it?" I had it. "Go. *Now!*"

I went, then. There were two more auditioners waiting by the door of the Downtown Studio, two young, fabulous types, whom I could immediately picture on MTV. I looked back at the audition area and watched as the other eleven people I'd been brought in with went out the exit. *Wait,* I thought, *is this some kind of a callback?*

It turned out to have been some kind of callback. In the room were three people I would come to know as the Talent Executives: Rod, Caryn, and Amanda. They welcomed me with warm smiles—it was still early in the day; my plan was working—and we chatted about my favorite bands, what I liked to do on the weekends, what kind of show I would like to host. Again, I have no recollection of what I said, but I know I tried to tell them exactly what they wanted to hear. A lifetime of anticipating people's needs and changing my personality to meet them was once again revealing itself as a job skill.

Amanda told me they'd be picking a top ten the next day and that if I made it, I'd be notified by phone by midnight. "And then the rest of the show will start on Wednesday."

The rest of the what now?

What the post on billboard.com failed to mention—because maybe it hadn't been decided yet, who knows—was that once the auditioners for the VJ job got boiled down to ten, the rest of the job application process would take place on live television. First, a panel of on-air talent, former VJs, and celebrities would narrow the field to five on Wednesday's *MTV Live*, and then in live events Thursday, Friday, and all Saturday afternoon, MTV viewers would cast their votes. My fate would be decided by stoned children. That this all made sense in the moment speaks to how deeply in shock I was to be in the MTV studios, gabbing away with talent executives and watching Carson Daly be all strong-jawed ten feet away, like it was all perfectly normal. "Great," I said. "Hope to hear from you soon."

I left 1515 Broadway and went straight to a phone booth to call in sick for the next day, so that I could devote my full attention to fixating on this. I called home to tell my parents about what I'd just done, and what Dad *thought* was probably whatever someone thinks when their twenty-seven-year-old son calls and says he has called in sick from work to stand in line to try to be an MTV VJ. But what Dad *said* was, "I have a good feeling about this. I think you're going to get that job." I have a good Dad.

That evening, I went online and checked my e-mail, which in 1998 was a thing you did a maximum of one time per day, and there was a message from my high school friend Ned, who had started a job at a magazine in 1515 Broadway that morning. "Dave—I work above MTV and they're doing some kind of audition to be a VJ. It is full of children and weirdos. I feel like I have to tell you this: If you're thinking about doing it, don't. The potential for embarrassment is high." He wasn't wrong.

I was living in a railroad apartment with Aimee and Louise—the one who had started all of this by making the wild suggestion that a person should love what they do for a living—at the time, and they were traveling for work, so I had the place all to myself. I bought a bottle of red wine, grabbed a full pepperoni pie from Original Ray's Pizza, and rented *Wings of Desire,* as I recall, so that if anyone asked if I'd seen *City of Angels,* I could say: "No, but I have seen the original German version." (If you run into the twenty-seven-year-old version of me, you have my permission to punch him.) I took the phone off the end table and put it in my lap. If anyone were to call, I decided I would give it two rings. No, three. Three seemed cooler.

By 11:45 p.m. Tuesday, nobody had called.

I'd had two whole days—and an entire German art film I wasn't paying attention to—to get accustomed to the idea that nobody would be calling, so it wasn't a shock, but rather a dull ache. A hunger pang. But somehow, I still felt inspired.

I pulled out my purple MacBook, opened Word, and began a journal entry about it.

Because here was the thing: I wanted the job—of course I wanted the job, who doesn't want that job?—but having been there, even for just fifteen minutes or two hours or whatever it was, had lit a fire under me. I had somehow reached the age of twenty-seven—four years of which I'd spent in New York City—without meeting very many people who loved what they did. I'd somehow heard the phrase "show business" a million times without hearing the word "business." It had escaped my understanding that if you have a passion, even if that passion is pop culture or music videos or doll clothing or whatever thing you love that the world tells you is frivolous, there is a business built around it. People make money doing it or planning it or writing about it. There is a place for you and for me. Being in that studio had jolted me to life. I felt like Gonzo after having visited the stratosphere via balloon. I was going to go back there someday.

"So I didn't get a call," I wrote. "But I've decided that it's okay because starting right now, I a . . ."

The journal entry ends right there. At literally 11:59 p.m. on Tuesday night, I got a phone call. I picked it up after one quarter of a ring.

It was Amanda. "Dave? You're not going to believe this, but you made the top ten."

Holy fucking shit.

I was to report to 1515 Broadway the next morning at 11:00 a.m. and expect to spend the day in the studio. There would be interviews, more things to fill out, and then a live show full of challenges after which they'd choose the top five.

I walked ten laps around my block trying to get tired enough to go to sleep. No dice.

First thing in the morning, I called my boss and came clean. I had not been sick; I had been interviewing—I said interviewing, like it was a normal thing and not a giant circus I'd willingly joined—for a job at MTV. "I'll be there all day tomorrow, but if you need me to come in at night and get anything done, let me know," I told her. "Oh, no," she said, "We *really, really do not* need for you to come in."

Gigi, the maternal MTV receptionist, greeted me at the door to the studios and took me to the Green Room, where the top ten were gathering. They included a red-haired skater kid who called himself "Ducci," due to his resemblance to a young Danny Bonaduce; a beautiful blond pixie named Kiele who had answered on her questionnaire that she was voted most likely to become an MTV VJ, and brought in her high school yearbook to prove it; Danielle, an African American girl next door; a handsome guy named David who worked at Kim's Video downtown and loved to talk music, and who I recognized as my direct competition.

And then I heard the voice.

"Heeeeeyyy everybahhhhdy . . ."

It was the tall, emaciated model from the line on Monday morning, and she was a dude. She was a dude with a variety of scarves tied at various places on various limbs, with outstretched toothpick arms, with a voice like the child of Carol Channing and an automatic pencil sharpener.

"What's up? I'm JESSE."

Well, I thought. *We have a winner.*

I decided that my goal would be to roam the studio as much as they'd let me. To talk to as many people as I could. To see who does what and where I'd be useful. To treat it like a job interview that just happens to air live on MTV.

At 3:00 p.m., the live show started. Carson, Ananda Lewis, and a British guy named Toby Amies were the hosts. The ten of us lined up across the studio. At the beginning of the show, we went down the line, introduced ourselves, and told Carson our favorite songs. Mine was "Philosophy" by Ben Folds Five. I think it was true, but more important, it felt on brand.

The entertainment for that day was a new pop group that had had some hits in Germany, and whose single "I Want You Back" was just starting to get some radio play: N'Sync. They were in oversized jeans and sweater vests with nothing underneath, as fashion dictated. Chris Kirkpatrick looked like a rasta pineapple. Justin Timberlake's hair was a blond Jheri Curl confection. I looked out onto Times Square, where two small pockets of fans stared up: a pair of German girls holding aloft a piece of posterboard on which they'd written "ICH LIEBE NSYNC," and a few older women with a sign that spelled the band's name out with the last letter in each member's first name: JustiN, ChriS, JoeY, LanstoN, J.C. (*Lanston?* I thought. *Lanston is not a name.* And indeed, it turns out one of the band moms determined that this last-letter-of-the-first-name-spelling-out-N'Sync thing would only work if Lance pretended his name was short for *Lanston.* So for the sake of a cool logo gimmick, sweet Lance changed his name to a name that doesn't exist. We gays are eager to please. Apologies to any actual Lanstons reading this book.)

The challenge, as I recall, was for each of us to interview Chris Kattan, and I'm not sure if he was trying to be difficult or if he was just on drugs; as I recall, it was rocky at the start but seemed to right itself by the end. John Norris was asked for his opinions after we all finished, and I think he mentioned me, but again, this is a happy, candy-colored blur.

Looking back, what is astonishing to me is that I didn't have a full-scale panic attack on live television, the way I almost definitely would now. I think the truth is that the situation was just too bizarre for me to react the way I should have.

Carson read off the names of the top five: Jesse. Ducci. Kiele. Danielle. And then . . . Dave.

Oh, dear God. I called the office and my boss said: "We saw." There was joy in her voice. In the moment, I thought she might be happy for me, but she was probably giddy at the prospect of finally hiring someone who knew what he was doing, and not having to pay me a severance besides. We all had a big night that night.

Thursday and Friday, we were the guests on *MTV Live* again. I remember something about a shopping spree to the Virgin Megastore across the street. I remember them pulling a postcard out of one of those sweepstakes wind-up barrel things, and calling the name of a viewer in Texas who would be the wild-card candidate, and thus flown in to start competing with us on Friday. I remember giving some kind of campaign speech on a podium in Times Square, which I had written over beers with a couple of friends from my improv group the night before. I remember world-premiering "Push It," the first video from the second Garbage album. Mostly, I remember spending the day with production people, all my age or a year or two younger. Cool. Smart. Obsessed with pop culture and gainfully employed. It was possible to be all of those things at the same time. I was learning a valuable lesson the hard and weird and televised way.

Throughout, people treated Jesse like the alien being he was. He was eleven feet tall, he weighed eighty pounds, and he spoke in another language, for he was from the mythical land of St. Mark's Place. He was, in short, exactly what a stoned teenager who had the afternoon to kick it in front of MTV and vote for the next VJ could ever want. I wanted to win, but I wasn't going to, so the safe plan was to lose well.

At last, the time came for the big Saturday event, the four-hour live show. I talked about De La Soul with Dr. Dre and Ed Lover, calling their beats "stupid fresh" (to which they replied, sternly: "Don't ever say that again"). I practiced awards-show podium banter with Pauly Shore. I did a thing where I interviewed Kathy Griffin and she pretended to flirt with me, having told Carson that I was her type. Being fat and having woeful self-esteem, I assumed she was joking, but having seen the guys she's dated since, I actually might have had a pretty decent shot at Kathy Griffin.

Here's what I recall clearly: there was a game show segment where the six of us answered music trivia questions. I did well in this one; I had shown up because I was a music obsessive, after all. But here's the thing: I was carrying around so much shame for being a music obsessive, that I actually *didn't* answer certain questions, questions I absolutely would have gotten right. I saw the huge disparity in the scores on the monitor, and I thought: *this makes me look like a weirdo*. I threw a few questions—what other names are Paul Hewson and David Evans known by? *Bono and The Edge. OF COURSE THEY ARE BONO AND THE EDGE*, yet I said nothing— because I was uncomfortable knowing so much about popular music *in a contest of knowing things about popular music whose prize was a highly coveted job deploying your knowledge of popular music.* That's some high-level internalized homophobia in action right there.

One by one, the six of us were weeded out: Nelly the Wild Card. Ducci. Danielle. Kiele. Until at last it was me and Jesse. The two of us, Carson alongside with an earpiece.

Now, I knew I wasn't going to win. But I still wanted to win. And these moments, as we now know from shows like *American Idol,* are unbelievably stressful. They're glacially paced, and heavy with import. For the first time in this process, I started getting nervous. My heart rate accelerated. I remember drumming my fingers on my chin, as though it were a thing I did when I was nervous. I had never drummed my fingers on my chin. Nobody had, because it is not a thing people do. I had an out-of-body experience. I don't remember anything that happened in those few minutes.

But I have been told I did not win.

Jesse was whisked away to the Downtown Studio to get his oversized novelty check for $25,000 and meet a gang of reporters for a press conference. I was disappointed, but I went to my dressing room, wiped my makeup off, looked in the mirror, and said: *Keep it together. Go to the wrap party. Schmooze, get business cards, treat it like a networking event. Hold on for one more day.* So I did. I collected a stack of cards from a variety of production people in roles large and small. I got a lot of *tough break, man* and a smattering of *we should do something with you.* I said: "Yes! Let's do that!"

I then went and met the rest of my friends to get properly drunk at The Gaf, where MTV was on the television, and *Wanna Be A VJ* was being re-aired for the second time in a row. I arrived just in time to watch myself drum my face and lose. And then they played the whole thing again, and then again, all weekend long.

I had a sense that my foot was in the door, and that my job was to start pushing. My friend Mike, a guy I had watched untold episodes of *Remote Control* with in the late '80s, told me: "The mothership just came down to pick you up, Dave. Get your ass *in there*."

Starting that Monday, I went through the stack of business cards and started trying to schedule meetings. What I seemed to understand was that even if people say they want to work with you, they'll forget in seventy-two hours if you let them, and my job was to not let them. I figured I'd just keep trying until they either set a meeting with me or asked me to stop calling. I decided to behave like a benign stalker. I'd had experience.

The reason stalking is so popular is that sometimes it works. A couple of higher-up executives brought me in. Chris Connelly sat me down for a strategy session. I got a freelance gig writing on a weekend countdown special called "The Top 20 Summertime Videos" or some such thing. My boss was a brilliant writer whose immediate supervisor seemed to be a little sweet on her. "Let's have fun with this one," she said as we began work. "I'm head writer on this, so he won't read it. He'll just tell me it's great and then we'll come up with better ideas on the shoot day. Watch." She pulled the keyboard toward her and wrote: "The Backstreet Boys' 'Quit Playing Games with My Heart' video reminds me how much I need a good, solid ass-fucking." We finished the rest of the script, submitted it to her boss, who told us it was great, and we came up with better ideas on the shoot day, because that's the way things worked there.

After I was around the offices for a couple of weeks, people started to call me in to test for some of the new shows they'd be launching in the summer. One such show I tested for was called "Eye Spy Video," in which we'd play videos and then ask viewers questions about what they'd just seen. (An SAT reading comprehension section, but with Everclear videos.) It got picked up, and I got picked up with it. They offered me a probationary six-month contract. At the time, I was still popping by at my advertising job, phasing out of it and getting things ready for a successor who would almost certainly be better at the gig than I was. On a Sunday night, I got my files in order, put my personal effects in a box, turned out the fluorescent lights in my office, and said goodbye to advertising.

At 8:00 the next morning, a Lincoln Town Car picked me up from my apartment and drove me to Seaside Heights, where the beach house was that year. Funkmaster Flex was spinning. Beautiful young people in very little clothing were oiling up their perfect bodies to begin filming "The Daily Burn," a new fitness show with *Baywatch*'s Michael Bergen. An intern took my coffee order and returned with a nice, cold Dunkin' Donuts Coffee Coolatta in less than ninety seconds. Caryn said, "Welcome aboard."

I had stumbled into my perfect job. I had bought myself a new life. My world had exploded and the pieces had landed exactly where they were supposed to have been all along.

And I very nearly chucked it away for three more hours of sleep.

Notes on (Jesse) Camp

FOR YEARS after *Wanna Be a VJ*, every single day of my life, I was asked about Jesse Camp. Every single day. Like, if I left my apartment only once, and only to go to the corner for coffee, someone would ask me about Jesse Camp. In restaurants in non-English-speaking countries, someone would wave me over and ask me about Jesse Camp. Waiters, people in the next car over at red lights, the homeless. It still happens once a week, minimum. Was that contest real? Are you angry you lost to that guy? Is he really like that? The answers are: *Yes, not really*, and *still, after all this time, I honestly have no idea.*

One of the first things I learned at MTV was that my job would occasionally include the care and feeding of our Jesse. Everyone's would. He was like a visiting friend who got himself a little too drunk; he was entertaining, but he could break something or wander off at any minute. If I was a little disappointed to lose the job to him, the Talent Department was straight up confused and frightened. Like, who is this guy, and how exactly do you take care of him? What does he eat? *Does* he eat? What, if anything, is he on? Who's going to get him to work?

Most pressingly: Is he always going to be like this?

I have no idea what he's like now, but I am here to tell you: For the time that we worked together, Jesse was really like that. Jesse was like that *all the time.* If there was a deeper Jesse, we never saw or heard him. It became something of a game among Carson, Caryn, the PAs, and myself: Who could catch Jesse talking like a regular person, and how would it sound if we did? We were in a time before cell phones had cameras or even rudimentary sound recording devices on them, so it would be tough to prove. Some of the production guys got the idea to bring a camera into the green room as he slept, hide it discreetly, and then do something to startle him awake and catch him before he was aware enough to play the character. But it didn't work, largely because once he was asleep, nothing we could do would wake him up, so after a couple of minutes the game would evolve into "Let's Make Sure Jesse Is Breathing."

My theory about Jesse is that he made a face and it stuck. We all learned at around the same time that he was not in fact a street kid, that like most of the kids who begged for change down on St. Mark's Place, he had a perfectly nice family up in Connecticut and had graduated from one of those ritzy private boarding schools. It seems to me like he was going through a kind of glammy, rebellious phase at age eighteen, the proper time to do those kinds of things. (I had worn color-block button-downs and cowboy boots during the 1992 summer of Garth Brooks, so I knew regrettable phases.) Right in the middle of it, he became very famous, and now he's frozen that way. If the cameras hadn't caught him, he might have been finished with all of this and well on his way to a prosperous career at Bear Stearns by nineteen. The world will never know.

The good thing about losing the contest to Jesse and then being brought around to do some on-air stuff is that I benefitted from the comparison. Jesse was without a doubt a big presence. He was a person you could talk about and speculate on, a guy who could render a group of teenage girls instantly batshit. I wasn't those things, but I could get to work on time and say words. I looked like Walter Cronkite in cargo pants next to him. Some of the on-camera stuff Jesse was supposed to do got funneled my way, just because the production crew figured they'd have a better chance of getting it done on time. And things that weren't supposed to exist at all—like *Lunch with Jesse*, a daily show where he got to just talk about whatever with whomever— got greenlit and fast-tracked. We both won. (Mostly him, because I actually lost.)

There were out-of-town shoots and events, and we traveled together a good amount, me and Jesse (and Caryn, and a minder, and Jesse's manager). It is impossible not to attract attention when you are with Jesse Camp, because he is an eight-foot-tall troll doll who shouts. I remember a layover at O'Hare Airport in Chicago, in which Jesse folded his whole body up like origami to actually use a single airport seat as a bed. We had just eaten a hangover lunch at the airport McDonald's, and his half-eaten Big Mac and fries lay on the seat next to him, just over his head. A pair of thirteen-year-old girls with autograph books silently, slowly approached him, starstruck. They took one step toward him, and then two, and just as they were within a yard of him, he unfolded and sat up quickly, opened his McDonald's bag, vomited into it, closed it back up, refolded his body, and went back to peaceful sleep. And then Caryn woke him up and walked him to the men's room: "Wash your mouth! You get in there and don't come out until you have washed your mouth!" The girls watched all of this in silent amazement, and then looked at me. I said, "Yeah." Caryn asked the girls if they wanted my autograph, and they were like: "No, that's okay."

At the end of his MTV career, as he readied the release of *Jesse & The 8th Street Kidz*, I actually began to feel sad that he was leaving. He was a character all right, but a good soul. A decent person. We went on one last trip from coast to coast for

Wanna Be A VJ Too, and my mood was spiked with melancholy. *He's off to become a rock star,* I thought, *but I'll always cherish the moments we had.* We sat side by side on our final flight together, from Chicago to New York, and I thought: *I might actually miss this person.* And we both drifted off to sleep, dreaming of our new lives: me with a new multi-year contract with the network, him with an album on his way and a tour to plan. We'd come a long way together, he and I.

Because the thing about Jesse is that he is pure of heart. He is a person who got massive, blinding, nationwide attention when he was a teenager, a fate I would not wish on my worst enemy. He was a good kid and I wished the best for him. (I still do.)

And then in the middle of the flight, he tried to climb over me to get to the bathroom, spindly spider limbs gripping the seatback and the armrests so as not to wake me, but something slipped and sent the whole situation tumbling down. And in the same instant, Jesse stepped on my foot, knocked my glass of red wine into my lap, and broke wind directly into my open mouth.

Goodbye, Jesse Camp.

13

A Life of Possibilities

THE WEIRDEST THING ABOUT WORKING IN TELEVISION was that I was the only one who thought it was weird. Carson could grab a mic and talk to the audience like it was nothing. Ananda worked the room and dropped knowledge about TLC casually, naturally. Matt Pinfield was going to be sharing facts about Semisonic with someone, so he might as well have done it into a camera, which he did with ease. Jesse was from another planet entirely, and everyone had learned to adjust to his rhythms, because it was obvious that he was never going to adjust to ours. I was doing the strangest and most exciting job in the entire world, and I couldn't say "Isn't this strange and exciting?" to anyone, because everyone else was used to it. So I just had to pretend that it was totally normal that I was suddenly wearing make-up and getting my clothes picked out for me and talking about 98 Degrees into a camera that was recording images that would get played in people's living rooms, sometimes right that very second.

Otherwise, I am fairly certain that I spent my first year at MTV in a constant state of shock. It's the only way to explain my lack of nerves, my even emotional keel, my sudden habit of saying yes to everything without thinking. And it started right away: as I taped the pilot for the show that would become *Eye*

Spy Video, my producer George got a call. It was from Tony, the head of production, and he was asking for me. It seemed that Carson and Ananda and Toby would all be heading down to Seaside Heights the next day to get ready for the MTV Summershare programming launch, so they needed someone to host *MTV Live,* the daily, ninety-minute live show from the Times Square studios. "You wanna do it?" Tony asked casually, as though it were no big thing to ask a guy who one month earlier had been standing on the sidewalk outside the building whether he could be the sole anchor for ninety minutes of live television programming. "Sure," I said, as though it were not a terrifying thing to do. "Great!" he said, and it was settled. *Tomorrow, I'm just going to be on the air, on my own, for ninety minutes,* I thought, and for some reason that I will never understand, I did not have a TV-movie nervous breakdown right there on the spot. It just seemed like the right thing to do.

My guests would be Doug Savant of *Melrose Place,* who was appearing in the Matthew Broderick *Godzilla* reboot, and Stacey Dash from both the movie and the television versions of *Clueless.* And then the rest of the time, I'd be doing whatever: taking callers, talking to viewers out in Times Square, just doing whatever we felt like on live television.

Hosting live television is a dream, in that it doesn't make much sense, it's nothing like real life, and you forget almost all of it when it's over. You have an earpiece deep in your ear canal so that the control room can tell you to stretch, or to cut things short, or to stop making that face. There's a teleprompter with your lines on it, or in the case of MTV, just vague bullet points so you have a general sense of what you're talking about. There's a roomful of production assistants and producers and cameramen and audio engineers and lighting guys and a stage manager and sometimes an audience and everyone's looking at you. As the show is about to start, everyone seems nervous; there is a palpable tension in the air, because anyone could fuck anything up, and if anyone fucks anything up, it's live, so there are no second takes. Of course, the person on camera is the only one who can *visibly* fuck up, and that's me, and I'm new here. Then they're counting down in your ear (TEN) and your heart starts beating faster and faster. The person in your ear says you're going to start the show into Camera Two, but then fifteen seconds in you're going to Camera One and staying there, until you move back to Two. (SEVEN) And you don't know which one is Camera One and which is Two, and then there's the one on the big swinging lever thing that you will later find out is called a *jib*, and is that Camera Three? Or is that Camera One? (FIVE) And also they're moving the news segment with Kurt from act three to act five. (THREE) Wait, where do I look? (TWO) Your mic is picking up clothing noise, so use the stick for act one (ONE). And you're on.

And then it's a blur of images and sounds—the face of Master P, that Wildflowers remake of that Bowie song, a viewer won a car maybe? In the blink of an eye, it's ninety minutes later and you're on the other side. You're sweating and disoriented and tired somehow, like you've just gone on a long road trip through a thunderstorm, and you say: "Again. Let's do it again."

That's how it went. I was asked to do absurd things, and I said yes, and they kept asking me. I showed videos in a musty Seaside Heights bar for *Eye Spy Video*. I asked my audience questions, and if they got them wrong, they had to do dares—like guys and girls switching swimsuits, or someone kissing a stranger. *Eye Spy* had actually started as a drinking game show where contestants had to chug a beer when they got a question wrong, and we did three episodes that way. Then Standards and Practices reminded us that our demographic was *children*, and promptly shut that part of the show down.

The bar at which we shot opened at 7:00 a.m., 365 days a year, and at 7:05 a.m., 365 days a year, the front half was crowded with third-shift workers and morning drunks. We shot in the back half. I asked the off-duty cop who doubled as our security exactly who the patrons of our bar were. "These guys are the people I had to arrest once a week ten years ago. These are the people who used to be the troublemakers," he said. "Now they're too tired." They also had children, so in mid-June, once school let out, the day drinkers' side of the bar was full of seven-to-ten-year-olds with rat tails and tank tops and angry eyes who played shuffleboard all morning until it was time to walk Mom or Dad home. Those kids are probably the troublemakers now.

I learned very quickly that the Beach House, which I watched and loved for its live performances, dance shows, and Jon Sencios, is just a set. It's a real house, but every room was either outfitted with cameras or repurposed as a dressing area, make-up room, or production office. We wouldn't actually be *living there*. I wouldn't actually be microwaving leftovers and splitting chores with Carson and Ananda. I should have known that, probably.

I also should have known that working in television means watching yourself on television, and watching yourself on television is like looking into an unforgiving mirror in a room where everyone else is beautiful. You see your dumb face and your boring hair and your idiot clothes, and you compare them against everyone else's and just think: *Something needs to be done here. This cannot stand.* Plus, in my case, the camera not only added ten pounds, it revealed the forty pounds I'd gained since college. Where I had previously only snuck quick looks into mirrors—only at the right time with the right lighting while I was wearing the right thing—I suddenly had to face the truth, in motion: I got fucking *fat.* Somehow a steady diet of chicken wings, draft beer, and sitting had resulted in weight gain. Luckily, there is a whole department of people who will fix your hair and put you in new clothes and make you look current and fabulous. It works for a little while, but then almost immediately you get sick of your new look, so you change it all up again.

You know how sometimes you go through an old photo album and you see a picture of yourself from high school, and you think: *What could I possibly have been thinking fifteen years ago when I wore those clothes and did my hair that way,* but you have enough distance to be able to laugh about it and maybe even post it online on Throwback Thursday? When you change up your look on television, by, say, growing out your hair and flat-ironing it and bleaching it so that it looks like you have just come out of some kind of hayride situation, and then you pair that up with the finest in 1999 Chandler Bing bowling shirts and baggy jeans, you get to have the Throwback Thursday experience *right away.* It was mortifying and even with the best style team on the planet—they tried, they really did—I simply couldn't bring myself to like the way I looked.

Falling in love with pop music all over again soothed the body shame. About a week after I got to MTV, the teen pop explosion happened, and even though I was fifteen years too old and 100 percent too male for its intended demographic, I genuinely loved it. We all did. To be in that studio, at the center of the pop universe, with all the screaming kids inside, and all the hundreds more screaming kids outside, as "I Want It That Way" played and everyone sang along, nobody could deny the power.

There is a name for this, and as best I can figure, it refers to Max Martin's Swedish heritage: Stockholm syndrome.

14

Too Close

ARRIVED AT MTV IN A TIME WHEN THEY WOULD RE-AIR their successful shows over and over again. And people would watch them every time. I would. I have the entire first season of *The Real World* committed to memory from all the Saturday afternoon marathons they would run in the early to mid 1990s. All you need to say to me is "If you from the Bronx, and you trying to go to college," and I will follow up immediately with: "You either trying to shoot that jumper, or you *buggin'*." It is etched on my soul.

Wanna Be a VJ ended up being the same way. Viewers seemed to enjoy the drama of it, or just liked watching Jesse in the moment. It's hard to say. But MTV aired it repeatedly, and people on the street just started to yell the words "Jesse" and/or "MTV" at me. It was their way of saying: "I recognize you from that time you lost a contest on live television." It was weird. The very morning after *Wanna Be*, when I went to have brunch with my friends, people started to whisper and stare and point. I don't know whether I was in shock or denial about what I'd just been through or whether I was just too dumb to understand how television worked, but I instinctively checked my zipper. I still do, if people seem to be looking at me. That's what mild television fame is like: it's like walking through the world with your fly down.

The thing about being on television is that on some level, people kind of think you're always on television, even when you're standing right in front of them. Even when you're *right there*, they still think you're a fictional character, or at the very least a person who won't have the reaction human beings have when strangers point at them. So they'll point at you. This almost exclusively happens when you are hungover or looking terrible or standing in line alone at Nobody Beats the Wiz, usually all three. They'll go: *Look. It's that guy.* And their friend will go: *What guy?* And they'll go: *That guy from MTV. The fat guy.* And their friend will go: *Where?* And they'll go: *There.* And they'll point some more. Right in your face! So close that your eyelashes will brush against the tip of their finger when you blink, which you will do involuntarily because there's a stranger's finger in your eye.

HIM. THIS GUY RIGHT HERE.

And it doesn't feel exactly right to speak to them, because they're not really speaking *to you,* they are speaking *about you in the third person right in front of you.* They are, in essence, watching you on television, which is probably enjoyable for them, but your problem is that you are a person existing in real life. If they would say hello, you would say hello back and have a nice chat and maybe begin a lifelong friendship, but they're talking about you like you're not there, and it's the '90s so you don't even have an iPhone to pretend to check. So you look around for things to be fascinated by: *What are those over there—composite video cables? For $9.99? That's real savings.* And then their friend will study you for a good long second and say: *Yeah, no, I don't know who that guy is.*

This is the best-case scenario.

Often what people do is tell you that they don't care who you are, as though you assumed that they were starstruck, as though it were an American custom to go up to strangers and tell them that you don't care who they are. Generally, it goes this way: You are out with your friends somewhere, having some beers and some laughs, and another group of people two tables over will notice you. And you'll notice them noticing you, because people tend to be louder than they think they are, and also when someone tells their friends DON'T LOOK, what will happen is that *everyone* will look, and then the initial noticer will say STOP STOP STOP much louder than they think they are saying it. And everyone will start secretly looking, but again, people's secret looks are much less secret than they want them to be. You can feel when someone's eyes are on you; everyone can. So there will be whispering and silent pointing, which I can tell you from experience make a lot of noise. You notice, because this is what your life is now. It is a new thing that happened to you all at once, like a fast-acting virus. And again, there's not much you can do about it, because nobody is actually addressing you.

But it's happening—the whisper orchestra is playing its overture and the show is about to start. And here's how it usually reaches its crescendo: The person in the group who cares the least about whatever it is you do you will approach your table and just start talking, regardless of whether you or one of your actual friends is already in the middle of saying something. And this is what they will say: "OKAY LISTEN I DON'T OWN A TV SO I DON'T CARE WHO YOU ARE BUT MY FRIENDS THINK YOU'RE FAMOUS SO WHAT'S THE DEAL, ARE YOU?"

And if they truly don't own a television, and they really don't know who you are, which ends up being the case fairly often—as it should be, because who cares—they end up saying it to your handsomest friend, the person who looks the most like someone who would be on television. And behind them, the table who sent this person over will be wildly but silently waving their hands or making the hand-across-the-neck ABORT motion, or just pointing at you more forcefully than before. Again, you're not supposed to notice this, but it's happening right in your field of vision: arms flailing, like Fat Albert and the Cosby Kids every time they heard something funny. And then your friends have to go: "No, it's him. Over there." And the person says "OH." And you say "YEAH. HI." And you wave over to the other table—*HI! HOW ARE YOU?!*—and you all realize at the same time that Carson Daly would probably know exactly how to handle this, but you sure don't.

My favorite example of this kind of public recognition came in Las Vegas, when I was at a blackjack table. There was a large group of drunk strangers in my peripheral vision having the grand debate over who was going to determine whether I was me (and also who exactly "me" was). And I wasn't going to solve it for them, because I was right in the middle of losing my money. And they weren't, either, because they were loaded. I could hear that they had narrowed my job down to MTV or VH1, which was a start. Finally, they deputized a tiny Long Island woman to be their spokesperson and she tottered over to me, just as I was about to ask the dealer to hit me, and asked "ARE YOU THE ONE WITH THE BALD HAIR?"

Am I the one with the bald hair? Let's break that one down together: I am sitting four inches in front of this person, with a full and luxurious head of hair. So, first of all, no. The one with the bald hair—and we have similar builds, I will grant you this—is named Matt Pinfield. Also, *bald hair* is not a thing. Otherwise, great job, stranger. (I'm still a little bit angry at this woman a full decade later.)

And then sometimes people will just actively heckle you. I lived in the East Village for most of my tenure at MTV. The East Village was at the beginning of its gentrification process at the time; the junkies definitely had the edge on the strollers for the moment. The kids who would roam the streets of Alphabet City were the children of the locals, the sons and daughters of the hearty souls who saw the movie *Kids* and said, "Well, that doesn't seem so bad." These kids had never heard of being polite; they would say anything, and say it right to your face. Another word for this kind of person is "asshole." Anyway: there was a kid who would haunt the streets of my hood in the afternoons, just as I'd be walking home from the subway. I'd be minding my own business, a block or two from home, and from a window or storefront I could never find would come a cry:

DAVE HOLMES YOU'RE FAT.

And he'd laugh the menacing howl of a coyote who has cornered a beagle. And his friends would laugh. I tried to imagine that his friends' laughter was the nervous kind. Like: *Hey, Coltrane* (this kid is named Coltrane in my mind, because he was being raised by unimaginative East Village jazz people), *cut it out!* But probably they were laughing because to teenagers it's funny to be awful.

HA HA DAVE HOLMES YOU'RE FAT. And they'd always be hidden. Were they in the frozen yogurt shop? At the counter at Pommes Frites? Up in an apartment waiting for me at the window? I never did get a look at Coltrane or his friends. And it certainly wasn't because my eyes weren't frantically looking for something to focus on.

Once, I was walking through St. Mark's, looking in all the predictably punk store windows and beholding all the young Jesses in their identical Mohawks and army jackets, when I heard my name: DAVE HOLMES. My core temperature dropped below freezing, yet I also began to sweat. Not today, Coltrane. *Not today.* I started walking faster. DAVE. DAVE HOLMES. By First Avenue I was in a full sprint. I reached Avenue A and started looking for a place to duck in for a snack and a beer, and to hide, when the source of the hollering revealed himself: it was my friend Matthew. Just a friend, trying to say hi. A friend I had a little bit of a crush on, honestly. "Hi Dave," he said. *"Are you okay?"* I couldn't bear to tell them I was being bullied by high school kids at age twenty-eight.

(I did a lot of thinking about whether to include that story. I thought: *Isn't that giving him what he wants? Won't it satisfy him to know he's still inside my head after all these years?* But then I thought: *Maybe he's dead,* and the thought gave me such comfort.)

The most alarming development in my first year at MTV was the degree to which my fame went to my mother's head. Immediately after I started getting regular on-air spots, my mom began approaching strangers who appeared to be in the MTV demographic, telling them she's my mother and asking whether they'd like a signed picture. (They always declined. This did not stop her.) That first Christmas after *Wanna Be a VJ,* I went home to St. Louis for Christmas, and I was barely in the door before my mom said: "Okay, when do you want to go to the mall for the annual Picking Out of the Gifts?" I generally do not let an opportunity for free things pass me by, so we hopped in the car and went. And what several years in New York had made me forget about malls is that they're full of teenagers, traveling in packs. My mother walked a couple of paces behind me, and I began to notice that if a group of teenagers looked my way and lowered their voices, she would wave to get their attention, nod slyly, and mouth the words: *"That's him."* And then I remembered: we have never actually done an annual Picking Out of the Gifts. She just wanted to get my face out into the public. I'd been used. I should have been angry, but it was sweet, and also I was actively soliciting ideas on to handle the newfound attention.

But over time, I got used to it. I started to learn the things to say, the way to hold a conversation with a stranger, the proper methods for starting and ending an encounter. A couple of years in, I was feeling like a pro. And for the third *Wanna Be A VJ*, we ended up going coast to coast: Los Angeles, Charlotte, and St. Louis. My hometown! We set up stations down at Union Station, by then a thriving mall and a hub for the new light-rail system everyone was afraid to take, and I worked the crowd like the conquering hero I felt myself to be. *Maybe the next VJ will come out of this crowd*, I thought to myself. *And maybe we'll relate to one another and be friends and I'll finally be able to say: "Isn't this weird?" to someone and have them get it.*

And then I got an idea. We'd have ninety minutes off for lunch, and Priory was only a twenty-minute drive away. Let's go there with a camera crew and me holding a microphone with an MTV cube on it, I thought, and we'll just break into the middle of a school day on a hot afternoon at the end of the spring semester. The kids will go bananas. I will be carried on the shoulders of students and faculty alike. It will be great television. I called the headmaster's office and spoke to his assistant: "Hey! It's me, Dave Holmes!" (Pause.) "Class of '89!" (Pause.) "Anyway, may I speak with Father Gregory?" She connected me, and I spoke with Father Gregory and told him what we're planning on doing, and he seemed enthusiastic— but I might just have been projecting. He told me Father Paul was teaching Honors Calculus, and I said "Perfect, we will break in on Father Paul's Honors Calculus class. This is going to be *amazing.*" And we showed up on campus, loaded the cameras, and stealthily mic'd me up in the parking lot. Then I led the crew into the main building and up to the second floor, right to where I used to take Father Paul's classes, and I busted in, yelling "WHAT'S UP, PRIORY?!?"

The kids looked at me, and then back at Father Paul, and then back at me, and they said: "Oh. Hi." And then they turned back to Father Paul, who was in the middle of explaining some calculus thing. It was not the enthusiastic welcome I was expecting, but then I remembered the Honors kids from my class were kind of wallflowers, so I kept going classroom-to-classroom, and kept getting the same response. It might actually have been great television, but for none of the reasons I was picturing, and I thank God we didn't do any of it live.

We didn't end up getting anyone to pretend they were happy to see me, and I tried desperately to put a good face on it, my smile beaming like I'd just had a wonderful time, as the camera guys unloaded and the sound guy took my mic off my shirt. Just then, Mr. Gleich, my old Dean of Students, came out of the building: "Dave! Dave Holmes!" He came toward me, and I gave him a huge hug, because I'd always liked him and also because I needed a hug. "It's good to see you," he told me as he hugged back. And then he whispered, right into my ear: "Check your zipper."

Sometimes mild television fame *actually is* walking through the world with your fly down.

Eventually, I got over my self-consciousness and was ready to mingle with my public. One afternoon, two women outside the studio approached me and said, "We're sorry to bother you, but would you mind taking a picture?" "Sure," I answered with a smirk. *Of course they want a picture with you,* I thought. *You're on TV and they like you. Relax and enjoy it, Dave Holmes. You're a star.*

The two women squared themselves up with the *TRL* studio right behind them, fixed their hair, and handed me the camera.

The Ten Most Important Videos from My Tenure at *TRL*

10. "Nookie"—Limp Bizkit

This is a song and a video that are significant because they are terrible, yet the kids ate them both up. The deal with *TRL* around the turn of the millennium was this: the girls tuned in for the boybands, and the boys repped for *whatever wasn't that*. Sometimes whatever wasn't that was Sugar Ray. Sometimes whatever wasn't that was Dr. Dre. But mostly, the official opposition party to the teen pop explosion was the noise Korn and Limp Bizkit made. It was sludgy and dumb and the young girls hated it, which made the young boys love it all the more. It was never dumber than in "Nookie," in which Fred Durst invites you to put cookies in your ass for reasons that are never fully explained. It hung around on the charts forever. Nobody ever went broke overestimating teenage boys' needs to upset their little sisters.

9. "Say My Name"—Destiny's Child

This video happened right when Matthew Knowles got in there and started making some personnel changes. Just as we were starting to learn the names of the ones who were not Beyoncé, suddenly there were two brand-new Benoncés, no explanation given. None was needed. Here—put "Say My Name" on right now. Have you immediately launched into a series of dramatic poses on the nearest couch? If not, who hurt you?

8. "The Dolphin's Cry"—Live

Sometimes videos got onto the countdown because of actual grassroots fan support. Other times, labels were more actively involved; it was a good way to generate buzz for a new or struggling act. I don't know if the big labels had interns call and make requests, or whether it was just strongly suggested that if we wanted continued access to Everclear or whomever, we might want to play what they told us to. And sometimes one appearance on the countdown was all it took; once the kids saw it, maybe they'd like it and start voting for real. In the case of Live, they didn't, and we were asked to accept the fantasy that actual kids would pick up their telephones and ask us to play a long, proggy ecology song from a band whose previous hit came out when our average viewer was 7. (This one spent one day at #8. *Absurd.*)

7. "My Name Is"—Eminem

Eminem made his first chart appearance the same way Live did. When "My Name Is" debuted, none of us had heard of it, and we were in the nerve center. But this one took off, and I understand it, because it is a teenage tantrum in commercial-jingle form. It's abrasive and petulant, just like Eminem himself, and it still gets lodged in my head some terrible days. Em always seemed like a little bit of a jerk, which I guess we can chalk up to the drugs, but to me his worst crime is inspiring a nation of wayward youth to bleach their hair without first treating it with a rinse, causing the entire middle section of our country to be carpeted with orange Caesar haircuts in 1999.

6. "What a Girl Wants"—Christina Aguilera

The success of Mariah Carey and Boyz II Men in the early 1990s ruined singers for an entire generation. Suddenly, vocals became an arms race; if you weren't doing runs from the second you opened your mouth, what were you even doing? Better singing became *more* singing. I'll bet you nobody born after 1992 has even heard the National Anthem without the whole "Land of the freeeEEEEE" curlicue toward the end. Although Christina clearly had a voice, she also couldn't help herself but to beat you about the head with it. This is her at her most subdued, which is still pretty belty.

5. "The Hardest Thing"—98 Degrees

These guys were the only boy band that had actual, across-the-board sexual credibility; unlike the Big Two, you could picture any one of them just giving it to someone. It helped that they were a few years older than their contemporaries. It did not escape my notice that they all seemed to own a copy of *Form, Fitness, Focus: The Marky Mark Workout*. But really, their gesticulation game was on point—lots of palms on hearts, fists on temples, hands reached out toward the camera. They were performing lovesick kabuki theater for an audience of mid-pubescent teenage girls (and me). I interviewed them more times than I can count—98 Degrees was always down to stop by the studio—and once, my producer Don said: "Guys, I'm going to need you to squeeze in closer to Dave. Nick, you get on one side, Jeff, you're on the other. Tighter. Tighter still." It was morti-titillating.

4. "Blue Monday"—Orgy

I only put this on here because it is my understanding that Orgy used to be a hair-metal band in the '80s. Then they got kind of grungy in the early '90s like everyone else, and finally, for the late '90s, they went a little goth. Goth was a good move because it was kind of starting to become a thing and these guys were opportunists, but mostly because goth means make-up and these guys were *old*. I interviewed these guys before a concert once, and I saw them without the pancake, and it was like: *"Dad?"*

3. "Bye Bye Bye"—N'Sync

This video was the moment the band turned from boys to sort-of-older boys. The moment the label put Justin front and center and kept him there. The moment the rest of the guys sat Chris down and said: "We need to talk about your hair." N'Sync had weaker songs than the Backstreet Boys at first, but from the moment in this video that the song drops out for a moment and Justin looks into the camera and laughs, it was clear who would be running things in 2000. I knew every move from this video and broke them out a *lot*. Everyone at the network did. We were grown-ups. It didn't matter.

2. "Baby One More Time"—Britney Spears

I think I was the one who interviewed Britney the first time she came into the studio, but I don't know, because a lot happened in those years and who even knows where the tapes are. All I remember is that the MTV message boards were all lit up about her before this video was even released. The girls knew her mostly as N'Sync's opening act and maybe Justin's girlfriend, and they had their knives at the ready: BRINTEY SPEERS SUXS! When I met her, I found that she did not sux at all, but was in fact a total pro: media-coached to within an inch of her life, a little dazed by all the attention, but talented. My agent at the time was a fan, and he told me: "I *like* that she's a little fat," and that's when I started to realize I might be in an industry that was fundamentally evil. Also, I have tried my whole life to look as cool as the first kid out of the classroom in the bucket hat, and I have never come anywhere close.

1. As Long As You Love Me"—Backstreet Boys

"I Want It That Way" is an obvious all-time classic, but this video set the template for all the boy band videos to come. Each Backstreet Boy is presented in a variety of attitudes and styles, each shirt is shiny, and each lip is moist. They are in some sort of casting session in a warehouse full of old cars and basketballs, being put through their paces by a very Amanda Woodward group of businesswomen, until the Boys turn the tables, grab the remote control, and turn the women into a bunch of extras from a *Buffy the Vampire Slayer* party scene. The dreamboat setting is turned up to its maximum here. One of my more significant *TRL* memories is seeing Kevin's eyebrows for the first time and thinking: Mister, you have my respect.

15

Unpretty

NEVER DID SPRING BREAK IN COLLEGE, SO MY FIRST experience of Cancun happened at age twenty-seven, when a person is much too old to experience Spring Break in Cancun, but years of watching MTV primed me for an experience. I flew down for my first one in the late afternoon in the spring of 1999, after shooting a few episodes of *Video Cliches*, so I didn't get to my hotel until around 10:00 at night. Right away, I saw the truth behind the fantasy Simon Rex had fed me for so many years.

As I checked in, a young man in a backwards baseball cap and a torn tank top with vomit somehow down the *back* stood wobbling by a house phone, trying to call up to his room. Evidently he'd lost his key or his wristband or both, and he needed someone to bring him up. After a few tries, he made contact, and moments later, the elevator door dinged and an angry Midwestern sorority girl stomped out. She too was unsteady from day drinking, her face puffy with tears as her bare feet slapped against the marble of the lobby floor. "You piece a *shit*," she growled at him as she stalked closer, "fuckin' piece a *shit*." She grabbed his arm and led him back to the elevator, sorority letters on the ass of her shorts fading into the distance. This guy must have flirted with another girl, or disrespected her in some way over the course of however many frozen things they'd downed, and now there would be hell to pay.

This is what they don't show you: the strained relationships, the anger, the consequences of drinking sugary drinks in the hot sun. It's ugly. I'd rather watch Jerry Springer. (Which would have been easy, because we brought him.)

It immediately became clear in Cancun that if you wanted to have a nice, calm drink with your grown-up friends—and talk, and hear one another, and not have anyone try to pour tequila and sour mix directly into your throat and blow a whistle in your face—you were out of luck. But, hey, a job was a job and a free trip to Cancun was a free trip to Cancun.

One day when I had neither an on-air assignment nor any particular desire to be on the beach with the college kids, I got a call from my production manager friend Kirtie, who was about to go on a location scout for an upcoming shoot. "Come with me," she said. "It'll be a fun way to see the sights." I agreed. So we hopped in her rental and saw the sights, or at least the sights that would attract young people, so we might as well have been seeing the sights of Orlando. We rolled up to a popular daiquiri place with a big stage, a view of the beach, and a disturbingly large crowd for 11:00 a.m. We went in.

A young bar-mitzvah-style DJ named Timbo took to the microphone and shouted "WHO'S READY FOR THE DANCE CONTEST?" We were not ready for the dance contest, because it was 11:00 a.m., but we were intrigued, so we followed the sound of DJ Timbo's voice. The place was arranged amphitheater-style, and the crowd fanned out before him. "NOW, TIMBO IS IN CHARGE OF WHO DANCES WITH WHO, SO GET READY TO MAKE A NEW FRIEND." Okay, this seemed fair; you didn't want people who'd workshopped a routine for weeks. To begin, DJ Timbo picked a shirtless nineteen-year-old boy from one side of the audience and a blond sorority social chair from the other. "Livin' La Vida Loca" played, as it always did in 1999, and couple #1 danced. Immediately, they ground their hips into one another, really letting the rum and sugar take control of their crotches. It was an inspiring performance. The crowd cheered. Kirtie and I smiled. Youth!

DJ Timbo pointed into the crowd once, and then twice, to select couple #2: a massive linebacker from some southern state school, and a tiny Italian-American spitfire from, let's say, Delaware. They bobbed up and down next to one another, and the crowd was tepid. And then their eyes met, their need for validation kicked in, and they chose to step it up. Football Guy picked Li'l Bits up with one hand and bounced her up and down. But the thing is: he picked her up by her undercarriage. He stuck one hand in her thigh gap and up she went, like she was a tray of hors d'oeuvres. Or really, more like she was a tiny painter's palette, because his thumb was pretty much right inside of her. Li'l Bits whooped, playfully slapping at his hand. "Oh, *you*," her laughing face seemed to say. "Get your hand out of my vagina!" The crowd ate it right up.

So obviously couple #3 was going to have to bring it, and Kirtie and I huddled closer together out of fear for what that might mean. DJ Timbo selected a guy in the board shorts/white socks pulled up all the way/flat-brim cap uniform of the Orange County surfer dude and a girl with the tight, oiled-up curls of Bijou Phillips in *Bully*. And as the song switched to Jay Z's "Can I Get A . . . ," Bijou made a brief show of bopping before pulling OC's board shorts down and putting his dick in her mouth.

His dick.

A stranger's dick. In her mouth.

On a stage. In Mexico. In front of two hundred hooting, slobbering, still-drunk-from-last-night college kids, two horrified adults, and DJ Timbo. At 11:03 a.m. on a Wednesday.

Couple #3 won.

The prize was a daiquiri.

*   *   *

The Spring Breaks, Summer Houses, and Winter Lodges weren't just opportunities for young people to molest one another, they were also chances for MTV to try new things, to produce specials that would act as pilots for potential future shows. If they worked, they found their way onto the schedule. If they didn't, they didn't.

If they really didn't, sometimes we faced legal action.

In the winter of 2001, we were on a ratings high. *TRL* felt like an institution, having been on the air for an epic two-and-a-half years. N'Sync and Backstreet Boys were selling a million records a week, and new boy bands like O-Town and LFO were plucking their eyebrows in the wings. (Boy bands were such big business, David Letterman had a fake one called Fresh Step that would make occasional guest appearances.) Limp Bizkit and Korn were still the inexplicable choices of the high school jock, moments away from passing the "rock band with a rapper and/or DJ for some reason" torch to Linkin Park, Incubus, and Crazy Town. The Corrs almost happened, for God's sake. The music business and MTV were flush. It was time to party.

We rolled up to the mountain community of Big Bear, California, for our annual Snowed In weekend with a bunch of ideas up the sleeves of our ski jackets. We'd do a mountaintop *Say What Karaoke.* We'd film a *House Of Style* special and show young women how to expose their navels in winter temperatures. On *Celebrity Dream Date,* we'd pit teams of girls against one another in a series of physical and mental and probably emotional challenges for the chance to go out with 98 Degrees. We'd also force one girl into an acting exercise, as she would be asked to appear delighted to be paired with Justin Jeffre. (Justin was 98 Degrees's bass voice. He would go on to run for mayor of Cincinnati, which explains why 98 Degrees always looked like three guys from a boy band and one mayor of Cincinnati.)

In one of the *Celebrity Dream Date* challenges, five teams of four girls would ride an inflatable life raft down the bunny slope to the picnic area, where they would grab a token or answer a question about Nick Lachey's ab regimen or something. I don't remember, but I do know this: when the production team rehearsed this segment, the bunny slope wasn't nearly steep enough for the life raft to pick up any speed. This rehearsal took place about twenty minutes before the show was scheduled to start, so we needed solutions and we needed them fast. A production assistant suggested spraying the bottom of each life raft with WD-40, and with the clock ticking, it was decided that that was absolutely the way to go. The teams of four girls ran to their rafts, hopped in, and with a tiny push took off exactly like greased lifeboats. The packed-down snow of the bunny slope and the dependable lubricative powers of the WD-40 proved to be a dream team, as five teams of four girls screamed downhill at speeds almost too high for our camera crew to capture, stopping not so much near the picnic area—studded with metal tables and benches that were bolted to the ground—as *in* it. They made impact in a cloud of snow, limbs, and ski hats that looked like a bar fight from an Andy Capp strip. Paramedics were called; bandages and splints were applied; and Nick Lachey was dispatched to the area to give hugs, defuse tensions, and gently suggest that nobody contact a lawyer. And the show went on.

The higher-ups at MTV especially wanted a talent and variety show, wherein contestants could show off their strangest skills, scored to the hits of the day. (And the stranger and more dangerous or repulsive the skill the better, this being the dawn of *Jackass*.) As with *The Gong Show,* a panel of celebrities would judge these performances. And should they deem one especially awful, they would pull a chain, activate a sound effect, and the act would be removed from the stage while the audience chanted the show's title: *Dude, This Sucks.*

Here is the story of *Dude, This Sucks,* as I remember it.

A bunch of producers had gone up to Big Bear early, to mix among the local youth and try to find acts for the show. Pickings were pretty slim: Lots of pretty girls who could Hula-Hoop and white boys who could freestyle. Nothing outstanding. No must-see act. And then they got an idea.

A month or so before, we had held our annual Sports & Music Festival in Lake Elsinore, a desert city where the extreme athletes would have plenty of room to do their tricks. I had hosted a special edition of *Say What Karaoke* there, and among our acts were two filthy, bony desert rats whose names I don't remember, but for our purposes, let us say they were both named Cody. Cody and Other Cody wore bleached-blond Eminem haircuts and A. J. McLean facial hair. They wore very baggy party trousers, had piercings in their faces, and had tattoos in semicircles over their navels, phrases like "Only God Could Judge Me" or "Thug Life" or "Who Farted," in calligraphy. I don't remember what they sang, but I am confident in my assumption that it was Papa Roach's "Last Resort." Cody and Other Cody were the reality behind the character of Jesse Pinkman, and they frightened me, but they made for good television. (I was approaching my thirtieth birthday by this time, and things that frighten old people are by definition good television.)

Lake Elsinore was just a short drive from Big Bear, so a smart young producer named Kelly (names have been changed, for reasons that will reveal themselves long after any sensible person will have stopped reading) called one of the Codys to see if they'd be interested in doing an act for the show. "Do you have any crazy talents?" she asked.

Cody demurred, "Not really, yo."

"Are you sure?" Kelly said.

"Nah, I mean . . ."

"You could do anything. Be crazy!"

"Well . . ." Cody confided, "sometimes I do this thing where I put my asshole on the water jet in a hot tub and I fill my ass up with hot tub water and then I shoot the water out, and I can hit a target."

Kelly responded the only way a hard-working MTV producer on a mission to attract young eyeballs could: "Can Other Cody do it, too?"

Cody said, "No, but I bet I could teach him."

Kelly said: "Perfect."

The host of this show would be Kevin Farley, Chris's brother and a very funny actor in his own right, who was currently starring as the Justin Jeffre of MTV's parody boy band "2Gether." (Kevin has since turned his attention to conservative comedy, having recently appeared as a combination of Michael Moore and Ebenezer Scrooge in the alleged comedy *An American Carol*. His swerve rightward may well have been precipitated by the events of this day, which, again, may God have mercy on you if you read that far.) Kevin had never hosted anything before, and this show was going to have a lot of moving parts. I was going to be the show's announcer.

More thought than you would imagine went into the production of a show called *Dude, This Sucks*. Each act would have to build, and each one would have to incorporate music. It was not enough for a kid to juggle balls; he would have to juggle two, then three, then five balls, to the strains of "Mambo No. 5," and his act would be called something like, "Flying Bega Balls." Acts needed to feel current, fresh, outrageous.

And so it was decided that the sight of Cody and Other Cody shooting water out of their anuses and hitting a target was insufficient on its own. There would also need to be staging, and it would need to match the boldness of the act itself. It would go like this: two people on stage would be roasting marshmallows over a campfire. There would be a sign a few feet away from them that would say, in large letters: "NO OPEN FLAMES." Cody and Other Cody would make their entrance in park ranger uniforms with tear-away bottoms, shake an admonishing finger at the rule-flouting campers, and then they would tear away the bottoms of their uniforms and extinguish the fire with the water that they had brought onstage inside their bodies. This would be set to the Bloodhound Gang hit "Fire Water Burn." The act would be called "The Shower Rangers."

Now, I was only peripherally involved with *Dude, This Sucks*, but when I saw the description of this act in the show's breakdown, I thought, "Oh, this cannot be." I asked a producer whether I had really just read what I had just read. "I know, right?" she said with pride. "That's our opener."

The whole production department was in Big Bear for *Snowed In*, and this show was the last thing we were shooting, so everyone was hanging out backstage. Shortly before the show started, I caught the eye of a higher-up person in production, and I asked him whether we were actually going to do what we were actually going to do. He said, "Can you believe it?" I agreed that I could not.

I believe I had a reputation as a little bit of a pill back then, and I absolutely deserved it. I would write e-mails complaining about spelling errors in the lyric crawl on *Say What Karaoke*. I would physically correct grammar issues on cue cards. I have never complained about the size of my dressing room, but you will not confuse "your" with "you're" while I have anything to say about it. (Even if it's on a teleprompter and nobody will see it but me, *I'll know*.) So when another even higher-up executive swung through backstage and I simply pointed at the "Shower Rangers" entry on the show's breakdown with an incredulous look on my face, that production executive did not engage. He simply gave a thumbs up. This was going to happen.

Dude, This Sucks opened with all of the acts parading through the crowd and into a holding area stage left. As the show progressed, Kevin was to call them one by one, and each would try their best to impress a judging panel of early 2001's hottest young celebrities (I can't remember who, but imagine people like Jesse Metcalfe from *Passions*, Samm Levine from

Freaks and Geeks, and model Jaime King; again, very soon you will understand why nobody has rushed forward to attach their name to this show). Cody and Other Cody were front and center in the stage-left holding area, ready to do their bit for forest safety with a special secret that only they and we knew about.

Like, *really* ready. Like, ass-full-of-water ready.

It was then that a much higher-up executive popped in. I was relieved; surely a clearer head would finally prevail.

I said, "Hey, are you aware that two guys are going to shoot water out of their asses and put out a fire on stage in just a few moments in front of a live audience?"

He said: "Are you serious?"

I said. "I am serious. In fact, it is the very first act in the show."

"Wow."

"I know."

"Well, that can't happen."

"I *know.*"

"That's our closer." And then he boss took the show breakdown from my hand and sprinted to the control room to move the Shower Rangers from the top of the show to the very bottom.

Hosting a show like *Dude, This Sucks* is a difficult thing. You want to keep the energy up. You are wearing an earpiece and producers are shouting direction directly into your head while you're shouting copy off a teleprompter and calculating scores in your head. There is a live audience that is staring right at you in silence during the inevitable and interminable production delays. If you are on a mountaintop in California in February, it is cold. It is a challenge even if you've done it a hundred times before. Kevin Farley had done it zero times before. And though he did a hell of a job, he still blew a few lines and missed a few cues, the way one does the first time one does a thing like this. And though our production people were the best in the business, this was the first time any of us were doing this show. We all made mistakes. We all caused slowdowns.

The result was that Cody and Other Cody were being held stage left, with asses full of hot-tub water for the duration of a thirty-minute show that stretched into an hour, and then two.

And then three, and then more.

My final responsibility as announcer was to welcome the audience back to *Dude, This Sucks* at the beginning of act three, the last segment of which would be the Shower Rangers, whose performance I was now morbidly curious to watch. I stumbled a little on the intro. We had to do it again. Kevin flubbed a line or two. After what seemed like a long time to even those of us with nothing inside our asses, we reached the grand finale. Kevin called their name. The cameras cut. The marshmallow-roasters hit the center of the proscenium, and PAs brought the tiny pile of fake wood and Sterno out to the lip of the stage and tried to light it. And then tried again. And then tried again. Cody and Other Cody were so close to being allowed to release the water in their asses, yet still so far.

At last: ignition. The cameras rolled. "Fire Water Burn" played. The Shower Rangers, faces flush with a unique blend of pride, stage fright, and whatever emotion you're feeling when you're about to go number two in front of a live audience, approached the campers. The Shower Rangers pointed at the NO OPEN FLAMES sign and wagged their fingers no. And then the Shower Rangers tore away their pants and crouched. The fire was extinguished. The crowd rejoiced. The judges let the whole moment play out. Holy shit.

And this is where the genius of the MTV production staff comes in: the whole thing was camera-staged in such a way that the heads of the campfire people obscured the actual assholes. So you could see what was happening, but you couldn't really *see what was happening.* It was theater of the mind. And it worked. A victory for the Shower Rangers.

This is when I decided to leave. I said goodbye, I got into my rental car, and I drove all the way back to Los Angeles, very quickly, without stopping. You would have, too.

So I didn't find out until a few days later what happened.

This is what I am told happened:

By the time of their debut, what was in the asses of the Shower Rangers was no longer water. Even the most skilled of rectal sharpshooters is no match for Mother Nature, and in retrospect, nobody really knew exactly how much experience Cody had in this department. (Other Cody, we should remember, was an absolute beginner.) Also, once something is up there for as long as whatever was up there was up there, it wants out. Give it an opening, and it will take that opening by force. So while it is true that the Shower Rangers hit the fire, they also hit other things that were farther away, things they never intended to hit.

Specifically, the Shower Rangers hit two teenage girls. Let's call them Caitlin and Other Caitlin. Caitlin's father was a bigwig and was therefore able to swing VIP audience passes for his daughter and her friend. A VIP audience pass gets you right there in the front row. Into what we may now call "The Splash Zone."

So there Caitlin and Other Caitlin were, two teenage girls covered in strangers' feces. I am told, and I believe, that they were not too psyched about it.

The production staff hurried out into the audience once they grasped what had happened, armed with towels and bleach and very hot water and a second goodwill deployment for Nick Lachey. And great attitudes: *Ha! Wasn't that crazy? Aren't you two good sports? Look, a* TRL *T-shirt just for you!* Here again, the MTV people are straight-up magical: I am told that once the girls had been cleaned up and apologized to and promised tickets to every single MTV event that would ever go down until the end of time, their frowns turned most of the way upside-down. Such is the power of the promise of an eventual audience with Nick Carter.

It seemed that the shitstorm had blown over, but soon enough, famous lawyers were retained. Tapes of the show remain the sole property of the California State Police. The Codys were taken from their homes and forced to undergo a battery of tests for a variety of illnesses, because if they were HIV-positive or had hepatitis, their act would be considered something like assault with a deadly weapon. (They tested negative.) The whole thing became a huge legal mess that towels, bleach, even Nick Lachey himself could not clean up, and while it did eventually get settled, dude, that must have sucked.

The show got picked up, was renamed *Sink or Swim,* ran for a season or two with me as host, and featured about 300 percent more Hula-Hooping, free-styling, and juggling. We left the butt stuff to Steve-O from that point forward, and you can't say he didn't run with it.

But it was clear that things were changing at the network. Music was becoming less important, shock more so. The producers were getting younger and younger. While for my first couple of years I found myself working alongside people who wanted to do their best and make exciting, unpredictable, memorable television, more and more I was meeting people whose highest artistic goal was to be friends with Melissa Joan Hart. The ground was shifting under my feet.

And like the Shower Rangers, I was starting to feel like I needed to go.

I'm really sorry about this chapter. Here is a picture of 98 Degrees for you to look at. Take as long as you need.

All Right, You Jackals, Here Are a Few Shocking Stories About Famous People

THAT LAST chapter aside, I am determined not to write a show-biz tell-all, mostly because there's not much to tell; if there were crazy cocaine sex parties when I was at MTV, I was not invited. But something has to get excerpted on *Popsugar* if we're going to make this book work, so, you know, *here*.

Kid Rock

At Spring Break 1999, a just-barely-pre-fame Kid Rock DJ'd the festivities, and at the end of a particularly long shoot day, a few of my coworkers and I relaxed in the hotel Jacuzzi. Let the kids pound liquor Slurpees at Señor Frog's, we thought, let's be grown-ups and drink wine in the tub. We were having a perfectly nice conversation when who showed up but Kid Rock, shirtless and in cut-off jean shorts, holding a bottle of Jack Daniel's. He splashed himself into our midst. "Where the pussy at?" he bellowed. "Ha haaaaa I'm just serious." One of the women in the tub said, "You're in here with women. Don't talk like that." "Whooo! Ha haaaa, that's cool, I'm just serious. Y'all mind if I smoke?" He pulled out a cigar and lit it before anyone could answer, which was really the only way he could have made himself less pleasant. Our conversation stopped, and one by one everyone left except me; I was not going to let him win this Mexican standoff. "All right, Holmes. Where the titty bars at? Let's go get some *pussaaaay!*" I said, "Yeah, no, Kid, I'm gay." "All right. All right," he said, "Ha *haaaa*," and took another long, sad pull off the bottle. "Whoo." You guys, I wanted to live in this moment forever.

Tara Reid and Her Friend

Also at Spring Break 1999, Tara Reid and Jerry O'Connell joined us to promote their new film *Body Shots*, which I never got around to seeing and neither did you, but any day spent around a shirtless Jerry O'Connell is a day well spent. This was the Spring Break at which Tara and Carson began their short, intense courtship by Motorola Two-Way Pager; they met on swings as reluctant judges on a morning shoot of a beach *Say What Karaoke*, shouting morning-drunk affirmations at each other over a young Joseph Gordon Levitt, who sat in between.

Tara had come down with a friend from Los Angeles, a woman who we guessed was a few years older, not because of her face or body—she had the lineless face and emaciated form of the Los Angeles wannabe fameball; whether she was twenty-five or forty-five was unclear—but because of her eyes. She had the jaded, weary look of one of the dime-a-dance girls in the Pat Benatar "Love Is a Battlefield" video that the Candy Store Boys and I had scrutinized in our youth. We guessed she was around thirty, but, like, a *hard* thirty. We'd introduce ourselves like "Hi, my name's Dave," and she'd just look back at us expressionless, like "What do you want *me* to do about it?" Since we never got her name, among ourselves we called her Hard Thirty.

Tara and Hard Thirty wanted to be where the cameras were.

They'd stumble out from the hotel, still drunk from the night before or getting drunk for the night ahead. They'd spot our camera setup, and they'd run toward us. What they would never do is learn that you can't really run in high heels on sand, so they'd fall down over and over on the way to us, a Pig Pen cloud of dust and glitter. And then they'd reach us, sand in their mouths and cigarette butts in their hair, and send an intern to Fat Tuesdays to get them daiquiris. (And God help anyone who brought them the wrong flavor. On day three, Hard Thirty accepted a drink—a big one in a two-foot, hot-pink plastic goblet—took a sip, grimaced, and said: "No. Different," before giving it back to the intern. "Different," she repeated, in the low, lazy drawl of the day drunk—vocal fry before we had a name for it. *Duffrunt.* Which I guess meant: "Go get me a different one," because an intern ran off to get her a new frozen cocktail. No *please,* no *thank you,* no *Oh, wow, it's 11:00 a.m. and maybe I shouldn't be behaving this way,* just *Duuuuffruuuunt.*) But when we would go out at night and kids would take pictures of us, Hard Thirty knew where the camera was, and she would pose: hip flexed, chest out, lips pursed just so. Hard Thirty knew what she was doing.

About a month later, a bunch of us were in the green room, and someone ran in with a copy of the *New York Post:* "You guys, look at *Page Six*!" He threw it down on the coffee table, and there she was, in her signature pose, on the step-and-repeat at some museum gala or another. Hard Thirty was a sixteen-year-old heiress and socialite named Paris Hilton.

Mark Wahlberg

I cannot claim to know Mark Wahlberg well, but he would come around the studio a lot, and if we passed each other in the halls, he would pull me aside for a private moment and say: "They payin' you yet, bro?" I would assure him that they were payin' me, and he would say: "Good. You got to make sure they *payin'* you, bro." I would say: "Yeah. Yeah, no, I will," and we would go our separate ways, and then the process would repeat itself three months later when he had something else to promote. I have no idea where he got the idea that I was volunteering at MTV—that I carried myself like someone who absolutely would have worked for free probably had something to do with it—but his concern warmed my heart. Much later, three or four years after I'd left MTV and moved to Los Angeles, I ran into him at Saturday evening Mass, and at the sign of Peace, he leaned into me and whispered: "Yo, *they payin' you yet, bro?*" It's possible that this is just a thing he says to everyone.

Johnny Depp

The 1999 Video Music Awards were held in the Metropolitan Opera House, which was a big deal, and my friend Tracy Grandstaff (the voice of *Daria!*) was the head writer. I'd never written for an awards show, and I thought it would be a good feather to stick in my cap, so I joined the writing staff. As the event drew closer, I kept getting pulled away to do events or live promos for the show, so I kept having to pass on the things I was assigned to write, such as podium banter for Gavin Rossdale and Susan Sarandon as they gave best Female Video to Lauryn Hill, or for Buddy Hackett and the cast of *The Blair Witch Project* before they handed the Best Direction award to the Torrance Community Dance Group for Fatboy Slim's "Praise You." But there was one assignment I refused to give up: Johnny Depp was introducing Nine Inch Nails, who hadn't performed together in some significant amount of time that were supposed to make a huge big deal about. It would be epic. Depp and Reznor: legends coming together, kind of. I was determined to make it great.

I spent time on this intro. Like, *a lot* of time. I incorporated song and album titles and lyrics ("They caught us all in their DOWNWARD SPIRAL and brought us CLOSER TO GOD," etc. *God almighty.*). I did a ten-, a twenty-, and a thirty-second version, just so Johnny would have options. Tracy looked over my work, thanked me, and we were off. I called my roommates, my immediate circle of friends, and my parents, and said: "I stayed up all night writing the words that Johnny Depp is going to say on the stage of the Metropolitan Opera House when he introduces Nine Inch Nails. Please watch." Sitting in the audience that night, I watched Johnny Depp come on stage and looked to the back of the house and saw my words in the teleprompter— *they went with the twenty-second version, okay, cool.* And then I turned to see Johnny Depp hit his mark, look at all of the words he was supposed to read, give a dismissive shake of his head, and say: "Ladies and gentlemen, Nine Inch Nails."

My consolation was that literally everyone I had told to watch watched and still called to congratulate me on a job well done.

Puff Daddy and Dream

At some magazine party—I want to say the reception for the "Hot Summer Music" cover of *Teen People*—I ran into Puff Daddy, who knows everyone's name and is always at work. "Dave Holmes," he said, "come with me." I like an adventure, so I went with him. He made the high-sign to a group of teenage girls in matching halter tops we passed as we walked, and they fell in step as he led us into a stairwell. He closed the door behind us, snapped, and said: "Dream, sing." The girls sang a bit of a new song I guessed was called "He Loves You Not," a pretty decent song with some interesting harmonies, and then they all looked at me for a reaction. "That's Dream," Puffy said. "That's my new shit." "Great," I said. "That was really good!" But what I was really thinking was *How awesome would it be if the door locked from the outside and we were stuck here together all night, like in a sitcom episode?* Puffy's new shit actually did pretty well: "He Loves U Not" and "This Is Me" both made the countdown, and then they vanished a year or so later. Everything Puffy touched briefly turned to gold that year.

Lance Bass and Dream

Lance Bass had his Y2K New Year's Eve party at the Hammerstein Ballroom just a few blocks up from the studios, and I was to broadcast from there. The guest list was a real who's who: Jamie Lynn Sigler, Chris Kirkpatrick, various members of third-string Lou Pearlman boy bands and girl groups who identified themselves by name and name of group, like members of some kind of pop military: "Hi, Mandy, Innosense."

Lance worked the room in a gold and black top, the spitting image of the Gordon Gartrelle shirt Theo Huxtable wanted, and billowing black satin pants that gathered at the waist and then again at the ankle, with massive slits along the sides revealing bare legs. It was the kind of outfit that made you say: I am looking at a future gay astronaut.

The décor was what you would expect from a guy who got famous in an Orlando boy band: potted palms and paper lanterns. And at each table, massive floral centerpieces sat atop giant round mirrors covered with fake Christmas snow. It was very festive. It was very *Lance*.

One of the live hits I was supposed to do from the party

was me at a table chatting with Dream (who for such a fleeting pop band have evidently had a massive impact on my life), and a minute or so before we were to go live, the camera guy removed the floral centerpiece so that nobody at the table would be blocked by it. This left us sitting around a big round mirror topped with fake Christmas snow. I thought nothing of it until one of the Dream girls—Alison? Joanne? Li'l Sneakerz? Who even knew?—took her all-access laminate, and absentmindedly, just as a thing to do with your hands while you're waiting to go on live TV, started pushing the fake Christmas snow around on the big round mirror. A pile here, a pile there, a big fat straight line right in the middle. The producer counted us in: 3 . . . 2 . . .

For the first few seconds of that live hit, my eyes are massive and I have a look of panic on my face, because I realized quickly that it *really, really* looked like I was at Lance Bass's New Year's Eve party doing a massive pile of cocaine with a group of fourteen-year-old girls.

Eminem

When he burst on the scene, people said: Here is a controversial white rapper who will change the game. I said: Oh, look, Carol Kane is playing a Ukrainian male prostitute. Obviously, the guy is very good at what he does, but he also showed up saying "faggot" five million times and wielding a massive, tiresome persecution complex. I mean: "They tried to shut me down on MTV"? When was that? I seem to remember us playing you once an hour and interviewing you every other week. While he projected a tough-guy image to the outside world, inside our walls, he was absolutely the kind of guy who would throw a fit if his bottled water was room temperature. I don't really have any inside scoop here; he just seemed like kind of a dick.

Tommy Lee

Sometime around 2000 I cohosted some Sports and Music Festival or another out in the California desert with Tommy Lee, who at the time was riding a post-sex-tape career resurgence. He had just released a rock/hip-hop hybrid album with Fred Durst and Lil' Kim called *Methods of Mayhem*, and in the rocker style of the day, was speaking at all times like a black character from a story written in a white-supremacist creative writing workshop: a lot of *crib*, a lot of *word*, a megadose of *yo*. He was also being trailed by some extremely tenacious groupies, who made Heather-Graham-in-the-'80s-parts-of-*Boogie Nights* faces at him and stared lasers into his legendary crotch. As we wrapped on the final day, one such groupie vaulted past his security detail and stage-whispered into his ear: "Tommy, if you take me home, I will suck your cock for twenty-four hours." "Oh, word?" he replied dispassionately as his bodyguards pulled him away. It immediately became clear that this is how people start conversations with Tommy Lee every single day.

16

Gotta Tell You

SAY WHAT? KARAOKE WAS WHAT TELEVISION PEOPLE called a "strip show": it would air Mondays through Fridays, and we'd record a whole season in three or four days. If *TRL* took a few days off, they'd clear its set out of the uptown studio, build ours, and we'd crank those episodes out, seven or eight at a time. Audience members who thought they were there to watch a thirty-minute show would be stuck in their seats for nine hours, so PAs would hand out Hershey's Kisses and Miniature Reese's Peanut Butter Cups to keep their energy up and stop them from revolting. We were quick and efficient, but even when you're working with the best people in the business, the whole thing can become a blur. You can check out a little bit, and forget to watch what you're saying.

In what was maybe our fifth episode on our fourth shoot day in a row, a contestant did a cartwheel in a crop top while singing Britney Spears's "Sometimes." As I congratulated her on her performance and prepared her for the judges' critiques, I said: "The straight guys are going to love you." Our executive producer said "Cut" into my earpiece.

I said, "Why?"

She said, "You said all the straight guys were going to love her. Just say all the guys are going to love her."

I said, "Really?"

She said, "Yeah. Go again." And I should have held my ground, but we had a couple more episodes to go, the audience was about to go into a sugar crash, and I probably wouldn't have held my ground anyway. So we went again and I said all the guys were going to love her.

I was openly gay at MTV, but on the air, I wasn't out. I played with it a little by making a point of mentioning how hot I found Justin Timberlake on the occasions when I hosted *TRL*, for example. But nobody thought anything of it, because finding Justin Timberlake hot was one of those things we were beginning to do together as a culture. I didn't pretend to be straight—I didn't feign attraction to Britney Spears or get all hubba-hubba toward Destiny's Child or make lewd comments about Willa Ford (and she *wanted* to be bad)—but I wasn't out.

I met my friends at gay bars, and I brought guys I was dating to events. I'm sure I even engaged in some kind of public display of affection somewhere, but our phones didn't have cameras on them yet and our culture had not yet embraced the idea that big fat nerdy guys could be gay too. Or nobody cared. Either way, it didn't register. I could have made it clear by saying "I'm gay" out loud, but I never did—not even during the endless discussions of Eminem's use of the word "faggot," where it would have been relevant and useful.

And the fact is that I wanted to be out, because I had needed someone like me to have been out when I was fourteen. If Kevin Seal had been gay and said something about it, that moment would have been a seismic event in my life. It might have sparked a conversation in the Candy Store that would have

saved us all five minutes of feeling awkward about ourselves. It
would have been an easy, important thing to do for the young
versions of me who were watching. So why didn't I do it?

Rod was the highest-up of the talent executives, and a gay
guy also, so I asked him about it early in my MTV days. Rod
understood the business part of show business better than I
did; he's one of those handsome, well-dressed, put-together
gay guys who always looks like he's a little bit disappointed in
you. "I kind of want to come out publicly," I told him. "I feel
like I'm hiding, and I don't want to." Rod looked me up and
down, and I saw him sizing up the spare tire, the inept attempt
at stylish dressing, the absurd Ricky Martin stripe of blond
I'd asked the hair department to bleach across my hairline. "I
think . . ." He paused, trying to say *no* in the most diplomatic
way, "I think you should be just exactly like you are." And
that was that. So I stayed exactly like I was, which was kind
of nothing.

MTV didn't really know what it wanted to be, either.
MTV prided itself on being at the forefront of social issues,
gay rights especially. And in many ways, they deserved to be
proud. Pedro on *The Real World* brought gay people—and
gay marriage, and AIDS—into people's living rooms in a
way no other network would have allowed. They included gay
men and lesbians and bisexuals on those *Sex in the '90s* specials they reran a million times. But beyond that, they were as
conflicted as I was. There were two all-gay episodes of *Singled
Out* that aired exactly once, late at night, and then were aban-
doned by skittish executives. We had a stretch of *Say What?
Karaoke* episodes planned with downtown drag legend Kevin
Aviance as a judge, and after we shot our first episode of the

day, a high-level executive—another one of those handsome, well-dressed, put-together gay guys—came down to the control room and ordered us to replace him. "Too gay," he told us. We had a reputation for being inclusive, and a shelf full of GLAAD Awards, but we had no real policy on the ground.

I brought coming out up again once I'd been there for a year or so, once I felt like I actually worked there and was not just some sweepstakes winner—okay, sweepstakes *loser*—who'd overstayed his welcome. "What if we did some kind of National Coming Out Day special?" I asked a couple of production executives. "We could get Rufus Wainwright, and . . ." and I had trouble thinking of a second name, because it was 1999 and who else was there? George Michael? Chad Allen? Fran Lebowitz? They seemed into it, but you have to stay on people if you want something like this to happen. And I didn't stay on them, because I wasn't sure if I wanted to make my sexuality the subject of a television variety special.

There was also the question of exactly how big a deal I wanted to make out of being gay. I wanted people to know, but the only way to let people know was to tell them, and telling them automatically made it a *thing*. To say I was gay even once, forcefully and unequivocally, felt like an imposition on the audience. (Years later, I would go on to guest-host G4's *Attack of the Show* for a couple of weeks after Kevin Pereira's departure, and I mentioned that my boyfriend Ben and I had seen *Looper* the night before. Later that day, a commenter said: "Dave Holmes needs to lay off the gay shit. WE GET IT, DAVE. YOU'RE GAY. FIND ANOTHER TOPIC." This is a reaction to my having said—during ten hours of television stretched over fourteen days—the word "boyfriend" *one time*.)

This is something straight people on television never have to deal with. Take this, for example: During the 1983–84 season of *Saturday Night Live,* the opening sequence featured the main cast interacting with the New York skyline, scrolling right-to-left like Super Mario Brothers. Rich Hall lit a cigarette off the flaming top of the Chrysler Building; Billy Crystal bathed in Yankee Stadium; Julia Louis Dreyfus re-created Marilyn Monroe's subway-grate *Seven Year Itch* moment and flew up into the air as an animated man on the Times Square JumboTron looked up her skirt. And then Gary Kroeger, observing via binoculars a tenement full of silhouetted women in various stages of undress, turned to the camera and winked. Dude *loved the ladies.* Here's the thing: not one person said to Gary Kroeger, "What we can infer from this opening-sequence moment is that you're heterosexual. Are you sure that's what you want to lead with? Are you comfortable letting people into your personal life that way?" At the very least, nobody ever said to Gary Kroeger, "WE GET IT, YOU'RE STRAIGHT."

(Talking about my sexuality in the context of work still seems self-indulgent, especially when what I should be talking about is that when I'm looking for an example of still-rampant heterosexual privilege, Gary Kroeger in the season-ten opening sequence of *Saturday Night Live* is the first thing that comes to my mind.)

Now, if we had had blogs or Twitter accounts or any way to connect to audiences directly, in our own words, I would have been out. But we didn't. In the time of dial-up, if you had a message you wanted to tell the world, you needed the press to help you. And if there's anyone less interested in a fat nerdy dude than a guy in a Chelsea gay bar, it's the press.

Finally, in 2001, with the help of MTV's press department, I reached out to the publisher of *Out* and *The Advocate*. "I'm a VJ on MTV, and I'm gay, and I want to come out publicly," I told her. "Okay, sure," she said. "Next time you're in Los Angeles, let's have breakfast." I said I would, and then I immediately booked a flight to Los Angeles. I struck while the iron was ambivalent.

The publisher of *Out* and *The Advocate* was a very sensible lesbian who showed up to our breakfast date in a smart car and ordered a bowl of muesli and berries, and I respected her immediately. I went through the story of how I got my MTV gig, what I was doing there, and how much I wanted to be out, how much good I thought it could do. She said, "Okay, then, let's do it. Let's do it in *Out*." I said, "Great!" We shook hands. "What are the chances of getting the cover?" I asked.

"Oh," she said, "that's probably not going to happen. To be on the cover you need to be handso—" and then she stopped and her eyes darted down to her muesli. "I mean . . . I mean, *I* think you're very attractive," and I thought, *Holy shit, all gay people can stop time.* "It's okay," I said. "I own a mirror." And we laughed, maybe a little too much, and that was that. We had made a plan.

It took a few months, because magazine publishing moves slowly and there was not yet a website on which to do any of this quickly. But it happened. I did an interview with a charming writer named Jeffrey. A photo crew came to my filthy apartment and immediately suggested an outdoor shoot, so I grabbed my best Clem Snide T-shirt and we clicked away.

My profile was to be in the issue that would hit newsstands in May. And in May, I went to my local newsstand and picked it up. The cover photo was of an underwear model in a baseball uniform holding a bat, at least semi-phallically, baseball shirt wide open, abs exposed. This model was there to represent an actual baseball player who was allegedly dating the editor of *Out*, and who had written an anonymous letter about his experiences as a gay guy in Major League Baseball. The letter was published in full, along with eight to ten more photographs of the underwear model in various states of baseball uniform undress. A few pages past that, there was an interview with *Can't Hardly Wait*'s Ethan Embry, who was then in theaters as Reese Witherspoon's sassy gay friend in the romantic comedy *Sweet Home Alabama*. There were three or four pictures of him with his shirt off, which I have to concede was an impressive sight. And after that, me.

You agonize over something like this for years, and then it happens and it's behind pictures of an underwear model who represents an anonymous baseball player who may or may not exist, and beefcake shots of a straight actor who's playing an interior decorator.

But it happened. I came out.

And nobody really noticed. I showed up in the bars of Chelsea like a conquering hero. Like, *here I am!* And nobody cared. I still couldn't get laid before 2:00 a.m. Fat officially trumps Timberlake adjacency.

But it felt good. It still does. It feels good to be an out gay television person. There aren't many of us, even now. And I have to hope that the fourteen-year-old version of me who needed to see himself reflected on television saw it.

Anonymous baseball player, if you really exist, join me anytime. The water is warm.

17

Any Little Town

EXCLUDING BABIES AND CERTAIN MEMBERS OF THE DE-mentia community, I am the last person in New York City to have found out about 9/11.

In the late summer of 2001, I spent a few weeks in Los Angeles working on a new game show for MTV called *Kidnapped*. It was a hot time for torture and humiliation on television: *Survivor* had just completed its third blockbuster season of starving its contestants; *Temptation Island* stranded young couples in fragile relationships on an island full of alcohol and fame-hungry models; and *Fear Factor* was burying people alive, dangling them from low-flying helicopters, and making them hang out with Joe Rogan. As ever, MTV smelled a passing trend and ordered itself up some. The premise of *Kidnapped* was this: a group of four friends would think they were going to compete together, but then on the morning of the shoot day, one of them would be taken from their home by our goons and held in a jail cell. The other three would have to answer questions about their missing friend and each other. If they got enough answers correct, their friend would be freed and they'd all win an all-expenses-paid trip to Cabo San Lucas or whatever exotic locale we could afford. If not, we stripped them bare and whipped them with reeds or something. It was a really magical time to be working in the industry.

We began a two-week hiatus on September 10, and I spent that day with Shane, a semipro beach volleyball player I had been casually dating. We walked on the beach, and he asked me, "Do you miss New York?" I said, "Yeah, especially with autumn around the corner." He said: "Autumn," and thought about it for a few seconds. "That one's *fall*, right?" Shane was really, really hot.

At the same time, I was trying to get myself on Broadway. There was a revival of *The Rocky Horror Show* at Circle in the Square at the time, with Sebastian Bach as Riff-Raff, Daphne Rubin-Vega as Magenta, and Terence Mann (the original Rum Tum Tugger, thank you very much) as Frank N. Furter. Dick Cavett, who was playing The Criminologist—you know, the guy who tells you how to do the Time Warp—was taking a few weeks off, and they were stunt-casting the role with a revolving door of New York City media types. I begged my agent to get me in. That afternoon, when Shane and I were roaming the Third Street Promenade, I got the call. "You start a week from tomorrow. Eight performances," she told me. "Rehearsals start tomorrow afternoon. Get yourself on a red-eye tonight." The moment felt very Neely O'Hara.

Sleeping on the flight was out of the question, even though I had a whole row to myself; it was all too exciting. I bought the *Rocky Horror Picture Show* DVD and watched it on my portable DVD player twice in a row.

I landed at Newark at around 7:00 a.m. on the eleventh, as excited as I have ever been. I remember passing all the people going through security on my way to baggage claim. I remember thinking: *I will never forget this day.* A new life was beginning!

I took a taxi into Manhattan and got to my place in the East Village just in time for my roommate Lee to leave for work. His girlfriend, Michelle, was still sleeping in his bedroom, so I whispered the good news and he whispered congratulations. We hugged and he went downtown to work.

Around this time, I started to get a little sleepy, and my first meeting with the cast wouldn't be until late afternoon, so I went to my bedroom to get a little shuteye. As I recall, this was right around 8:30 a.m.

At 10:00-ish, I started to hear a female voice in the living room. Michelle was very, very young (twenty-five to our twenty-nine) and had a habit of calling in sick to work, doing bong hits, and watching classic game shows on the Game Show Network all day long. We'd come home, there would be cold pizza on the coffee table, and she'd say: "You would not believe what Brett Somers said today." It's one of those things that's a lot less cute when you're not having sex with the person who's doing it. So when I heard the chatter, I thought it was either Michelle or Fannie Flagg, and I wasn't down to hang with either.

I was groggy and starting to get a little nervous about the single biggest event in the world, which was my tiny role in a Broadway show, and I vividly remember thinking: *I cannot imagine anything worse than having to talk to Michelle about* Match Game '76 *right now.* I rolled over and went back to sleep.

Sleep comes hard when you're just off a red-eye and there's nothing else going on, so I snoozed pretty soundly for the next three hours. At 1:00 p.m., I woke up again. Same female voice from the living room. *All right,* I thought, *I'd better face it.* I got up and walked out into the living room.

It wasn't Michelle at all. It was Stacey, the woman who was subletting our vacant bedroom while our other roommate Brendan was on an assignment out of town. I hadn't met her yet. I thought: *Oh, do I have some exciting news to tell her.*

And then I saw the TV. Wreckage. Confusion. Peter Jennings at his most serious.

"What's . . ."

"Do you not . . ."

"What is that?"

"Do you not know?"

"What is happening?"

"The Twin Towers have fallen down" is all I remember her saying and I remember hyperventilating and her hugging me and telling me everything that I had slept through, which by this time was *everything.* I got the whole story, all at once, while the World Trade Center smoldered two miles away: planes used as missiles, a terrorist plot, nobody is sure whether more attacks are planned, the towers burned for an hour or so before they fell, one after the other. And then, after we sat stunned and silent in front of the TV for a half hour or so: "Oh. I'm Stacey. I'm your roommate."

"Oh! Right. I'm Dave. Hi."

Our building had a roof deck with an unobstructed 360-degree view of the city, and Stacey hadn't been up there yet. We went up and looked. There was a massive dome of dust downtown where the towers had been. Gray and growing. A lot of people were up on the roof, including a few of my neighbors who had just walked out of the cloud. They were covered in it. Like bodies from Pompeii. I don't even know if they knew. (I do hope at least one of them got something close to a laugh at my expense. They had witnessed the worst terrorist attack in our nation's history and had half a day to process it and call their family, and then the dummy in 1C came up in his jammie bottoms, like: *Wait,* what *happened?*)

We went up and down like that for a few hours. Roof deck to TV and back. Just finding new places to say "Oh, my God."

The worst thing at the time was that you couldn't help. Nobody was allowed anywhere near what they were just then starting to call Ground Zero, and word was starting to spread that they were turning away blood donors. *They have enough,* we thought. But that wasn't it. They just didn't need any. Anybody who wasn't out wasn't coming out.

Lee came home around 3:00, and I don't remember which one of us suggested it, but it was decided that 3:00 was an appropriate time to start drinking. So we did. We went to 7B, which some people called the Horseshoe Bar, and began ordering whiskeys. It was absolutely silent in 7B, which it never is, especially when it's crowded, which it was. Everyone watched the TV in total silence. Ned came to meet us there. So did my friend Kelly Sue from my improv days. We didn't talk. We couldn't talk. We had our arms around each other, tight.

Every few minutes, someone in the room would remember a friend who worked down there, and they'd pop up and run outside and try to reach them. You'd have to try your call a bunch of times before they'd go through. Sometimes people came back inside looking relieved, and sometimes they didn't come back. You could see them get the bad news through the window, hazy with cigarette smoke. My friends were okay. Thank God.

By the early evening, the smell started to reach the East

Village. I had never smelled anything like it before. None of us had. It was like an electrical fire mixed with gasoline mixed with burned hair. It was people and planes and buildings.

The story goes that we were united as a country in the immediate aftermath of the attacks, but that was definitely not the case in 7B. Some people cheered when Bush spoke, some people hissed. When he recited that Bible verse about walking through the valley of the shadow of death, some people heckled. Kelly Sue heckled back at them: "What if this is giving someone somewhere some *comfort?*" When the newscasters speculated as to whether our military would retaliate, half the bar whooped and half pounded their tables and said "NO." The bar was turning into a Parliament meeting, and we had heard and seen and drank enough, so we left. We walked up to Union Square, candlelit as the sun fell, where people were writing messages on the ground in chalk: "USA!" "INTIFADA!" "PATRIARCHY FUCK OFF!" Everyone was already claiming this thing as their own. It was already a mess.

We kept walking, and walking. The only things open in the neighborhood were the bars and the churches, and they were all crowded. Someone hung a huge American flag over Fourth Street. By the next morning, a few chunks had been pulled out of it.

We passed Bowery Bar, where "Beige," the Tuesday night gay dance party, was actually starting, right on schedule. People were going about their business like normal, but in a state of shock, and so were we, so we went in. The DJ opened his set with Siouxsie and the Banshees' "Cities in Dust," which we agreed seemed a little on the nose. We left.

Kelly Sue had just quit drinking a couple of months before,

so she went home. Lee went uptown to be with Michelle. That left me and Ned. Again, I don't remember who suggested it, but it was resolved that we should go try to get laid. ("Disaster Sex" ended up being a real trend in the city that week. All sorts of random hookups and unplanned pregnancies. *Salon* did a piece about it and everything.) We went to The Cock, because it seemed like the right place to go for such a thing. I think we both expected the place to be crowded, but when we walked in, there was only a handful of people at the bar, two people dancing to Soft Cell's "Sex Dwarf," and, on the periphery of the dance floor, smoking a cigarette and holding a rocks glass full of some flavor of white liquor, with a single, perfect tear going down his right cheek like the Native American in the litter PSA, Rufus Wainwright. We left again.

We didn't know what to do but keep moving. By that time, people were starting to hang up signs with missing persons' faces on them. Like lost dog flyers. Like they thought their loved ones had pulled themselves out of the pile and were wandering the city. Like they were just lost, with amnesia, waiting for a kind soul to point them home. You could start to believe that, too, if you watched these people hang these signs up, if you got a good look at their faces. You could make yourself think: *It's good that they're doing this. It's going to make it easier for everyone to find one another.* It sobered us up. Ned and I went back to our respective apartments, alone.

The actual cloud reached the East Village the next morning. Everything was hazy, like it had a filter over it. A big group of us had dinner together that night, and someone in the restaurant dropped their fork, and everyone jumped. We all had private conversations about where we kept our weed and/or porn, so we could parent-proof each other's apartments in case anything happened to us. I called one of the producers on *Kidnapped* out in Los Angeles to see whether we'd even continue doing the show, and he said we would eventually, though the set—a bombed-out warehouse space—would probably have to be rethought. We talked about the whole thing for a while and he said: "A bunch of us went out for dinner last night, and the waiter asked if we wanted dessert, and we all just went ahead and *got some*. This thing is really affecting everybody."

The next day, I went up to the studio for the special *TRL* we did, and after it was over, I decided to get out of the city. There was nothing I could do but wander and sigh and feel heavy, so I just made the decision and was on my way thirty minutes later. I hopped on an all-night train to Chicago, walked to the first rental-car place I saw, and rented their last car, which was a red Mustang convertible. I drove it to St. Louis, hung around and hugged my family too much for a few days, and then drove the rest of the way out to Los Angeles. I had only the clothes on my back and my laptop, so I bought new shirts and jeans and underwear from Gaps along the way. John Mayer's *Room for Squares* was re-released by Sony Columbia on September 18, so I picked it up in a Best Buy in Texas and listened to it over and over again. ("Your Body Is a Wonderland" is indefensible, but the rest of that shit holds up.)

When I got back to my place in Santa Monica, it was exactly as I had left it. I had bought a stack of newspapers the afternoon of the tenth; I was either making a special effort to stay up on current affairs or just doing all the puzzles, but either way it was mostly to counteract whatever effect Shane was having on me. I had the *New York Times*, the *Los Angeles Times, USA Today*. And they were full of *nothing*. Stacks of pages of whatever we felt was important enough to talk about before all of this happened. They were like transmissions from another dimension.

I kept them. I thought: these will be valuable someday. These are the literal last messages from the old world.

I thought: *We will never be this frivolous, this silly, this unserious ever again.*

I think a lot of stupid things.

Rocky Horror came back after a few months, like the rest of the shows on Broadway did, and I had my eight performances, right after Cindy Adams, just before Sally Jesse Raphael. Sebastian Bach had his teenage son with him backstage a lot, and the kid had his nose in a book most of the time, and it dawned on me that that's how you rebel against your dad when your dad is Sebastian Bach.

Right away, I clicked with one of the chorus boys, a gorgeous Irish-looking dude with a beautiful voice and perfect hair and teeth. We went out for an early dinner between the matinee and the evening show on Wednesday, and while we initially couldn't get in at Ruby Foo's, a manager came sprinting from the back and said: *"Right this way, Mr. Holmes."* This had never happened before (or since, for that matter), and it could not possibly have happened in front of a better person. It was a sign. A new life really was beginning after all. And then we sat down and ordered our sushi and he told me about his girlfriend who was down the street performing in *Seussical: The Musical.* Even on Broadway, even doing a musical about the joys of bisexuality, I picked the straight chorus boy to have a crush on. (That chorus boy: Matthew Morrison.)

Kidnapped went through some changes, but it ran for a whole season. I went back and forth between New York and

L.A., each time bringing more of my stuff west. It was the last year of my contract with MTV, and I could have tried to get another one, but I felt myself getting less and less busy. I saw the new kids getting more and more screen time, and I couldn't bear to hear someone tell me that I was fired, so I said: "I think I'm just going to ride out the rest of my contract and then just move on," and Rod said: "That sounds like a good idea." A few months later the checks stopped coming and I didn't work at MTV anymore. That's the way it happens: your contract runs out and nobody knows it except someone in business affairs. You just kind of go away.

I found someone to sublet my room for a while, and his temp job in the city went permanent, so he could stay as long as I needed him to. There was no work reason for me to be in New York City. Only my friends made me want to go back, and with T9 predictive texting, staying in touch with them was a snap. Everyone was pairing off and growing up anyway; where a few years before we'd been together in every spare moment, we were seeing each other once a week, then once a month, then less. We were on our way to becoming people who mean to see one another.

I had a brand new city, full of new people to meet and jobs to get; the weather was perfect every day; and most of my belongings were already in it.

I never made a decision or said goodbye to anyone. I just woke up one morning, looked around, and said: "Huh. I guess I live in Los Angeles."

18

Such Great Heights

THE FIRST THING YOU REALIZE WHEN YOU MOVE TO Los Angeles, before the perfect weather or the traffic, is the enthusiasm. It is a happy bunch out there in L.A.; people have their little teas and go for their little hikes and they are *psyched*. There is nothing you can say to a guy in Los Angeles that won't make him answer "NICE."

"I'm going home to do laundry."

"Nice."

"Today is Tuesday, and tomorrow, it will be Wednesday."

"Nice!"

"I wear shoes sometimes."

"NOYCE."

It is as phony as it can be, but it is inspiring in its way, because it is no less authentic than New York's knee-jerk cynicism, and at least it makes you happy for a moment.

The hardest part about moving to Los Angeles wasn't starting over socially; there were enough former MTV people making the move west, and I got back into the inherently social world of improv right when I got there. The hard thing was starting over professionally. MTV gives a person a decent amount of notoriety, but casting directors don't like people with a decent amount of notoriety. Casting directors want to discover you, or they want to land a famous name. If you're in between, you have a tough road. You go out for everything, and then you lose it, either to someone you don't recognize who's five years younger than you or to a legit celebrity; but either way you spend time in waiting rooms with Danny Bonaduce.

Along the way, you get all kinds of great advice. Producers in casting sessions will say things like: "Our audience is *influencers,* so keep that in mind," or "Do it just like that, but better," or "You're talking like the audience is five feet away, I want you to do it like the audience is three feet away." Those are all real, by the way, and in reply to that last one, I asked: "Am I too loud?" And the producer said, "No, it's a relatability factor," and I thought *Oh, okay, you're just adding more nonsense words to a thing that already doesn't make any sense.* I did it again the exact same way and he said "Perfect!" and I got a callback. I think Alfonso Ribeiro went on to book that job.

Once upon a time, I got a call from my manager. I was new to Los Angeles, I was new to having a manager and going out on auditions, I was just *new.* He said: "NBC wants to have a meeting with you now. Now! *Go there now!*" *Of course this is happening,* I thought. *This is how it's going to happen. I am in Los Angeles and I am going to be a STAR.* "There's a new reality show they want you to host, and they're not telling me anything about it, but you need to get there now."

So I went and had a very nice lunch with some guys who at least pretended to be very nice people. We talked, and they said, "We have a new reality dating show with a twist, and we can't tell you what the twist is, but there is an element that you possess that is right in line with the concept of the show. We'd like you to consider hosting it." This was in the months after the first season of *Joe Millionaire*, so every network had a reality dating show and every reality dating show had a twist. I said yes, yes of course I would. *The show's twist is that it will be a funny show*, is what I told myself. *The thing that I possess that makes me perfect for this show is that I'm funny.* Now, nobody had told me this. Nobody said anything remotely like this in the meeting or in any of the phone calls I had with my manager. I just decided that it was true, and so it became true. I rolled open the sunroof on my Jeep Liberty, turned up the first Phantom Planet album as loudly as I could without compromising sound quality, and drove back to my tiny one-bedroom in the Miracle Mile. On the way, I passed the line for the *Tonight Show*, all those people in pantsuits and golf shirts standing around all day for the chance to see Jay Leno up close. "See you all soon," I said. I honked. I waved. I was ready.

I was a real asshole.

I had been warned that they had also been talking to "a name," and that this name was interested but might not take the job. If the name didn't take it, then it was mine. They didn't say who the name was, and I didn't push it. There is always a name. There is always someone who has had a successful run on a sitcom who would be happy to swoop in on your job and slum for a steady paycheck, and that's the way it goes. But sometimes they don't. Sometimes they go back to counting their money or designing their line of casual separates for QVC, and you get the gig. You never know what's going to happen.

I did a little bit of digging and I found out that for this show, the name was Kathy Griffin. *Great*, I thought. *She's funny. Like me. She'd be a good choice for this show whose twist is that it's funny*, which again is a thing that nobody had ever actually said to me at any time. I would be happy to lose this gig to a Kathy Griffin. We had a history, after all.

When I actually did lose the gig to a Kathy Griffin, I was less happy than I had predicted, but still, NBC had called. NBC thought I was funny, and I knew that because I had hypnotized myself into believing it. Things would work out. Back to the drawing board.

A couple of months later, I swung by my place in the middle of the day to make myself some lunch and watch *Passions*, a show that you needed to watch about five minutes of a year, because they were at the same party they were at last month, holding the same birth certificate, and swearing they'll tell everyone you bastard, dammit, they *will*. As I pressed a slice of bread onto the top of a ham sandwich, I heard the siren call that is Kathy Griffin's speaking voice in the unmistakable boom of a network promo. I ran to the TV to see a teaser for the show I nearly booked, the show I was perfect for.

The show was *Average Joe*, a *Bachelorette*-style reality dating show in which a beautiful young single gal shows up at a Calabasas mansion to choose a mate out of a cast of hunks, except the shocking twist is that . . .

Oh, *no*.

The shocking twist was that the guys were actually all kind of homely. They were all dumpy or overweight or aggressively hairy or just generally average, and the twist was that our bachelorette would have to pick a suitable mate out of a bunch of ugly guys.

And I possessed a quality that was *right in line with this shocking twist*.

It hit me, right there in my living room, ham sandwich in one hand, remote in the other: NBC did not think I was funny. NBC thought I was *ugly*.

Oh.

I turned away from the television and walked to my window to feel the California sun on my face, to tell myself that no matter what this industry thought of me, I was going to succeed. I might have to work a little harder, I might have to be a little smarter, but I'm going to make it fucking work, dammit. I *will*.

I got to my window just in time to watch my Jeep Liberty get towed away for unpaid parking tickets.

*   *   *

Having just come out publicly, I got a few auditions to play the gay best friend in romantic comedies and Lifetime original series. I got many, many opportunities to call the lead character "girlfriend" and tell her to *do herself*. These characters spoke entirely in catch phrases and had no emotional life of their own. They were to the aughts what the token black character was to the '80s and '90s. Once in particular, I went in for a sassy best friend role in an independent movie. My audition monologue was a speech the gay guy delivered to the main character about embracing her inner diva and getting *fierce*. The scene was to take place in the women's bathroom of a restaurant, just after the lead character saw the boy she liked having dinner with her rival. In the middle of this sassy tirade, another woman walked into her gender-appropriate bathroom—to use it, like a human being might—and my character said to this woman: "*Excuse* me, girlfriend, but we're on *official business here*," and then shooed her out. Like: *The ladies' room is for troubled women and their neutered friends only; deal with your natural bodily functions somewhere else.* Hateful.

I showed up to this audition, and it was a sea of skinny guys in vests and bow ties. It was a crowd I could not out-queen. I would have to change up my approach. I went in, I told the camera who I was and what role I'd be reading for, and when it came time in the script for the hapless woman to make the error of using the bathroom to void her bladder, I said "EXCUSE ME GIRLFRIEND, WE'RE ON OFFICIAL BUSINESS HERE!" in a blind rage. A deafening, terrifying, Vincent D'Onofrio in *Full Metal Jacket* conniption. Listen, you have to make choices as an actor. I didn't get a callback on that one, but I still think a sassy gay friend who goes into rage blackouts when women want to use their own bathroom for its intended purpose is a character in search of a movie.

Eventually I got a semi-regular gig playing a gay stereotype on Comedy Central's *Reno 911!*, and just before cameras rolled on my first day of shooting, Thomas Lennon—in mustache and tiny khaki shorts—assuaged my fear about playing such a character: "Just remember, Dave, we are all playing terrible, terrible people." It is the most freeing thing I have ever heard on a set, bar none.

The audition process for *Reno 911!* was, without a doubt, the most fun you could have in an audition, which I understand is not saying much. I begged my manager to get me in the room, and he did, and I prepared a character and a situation, as the casting director told me to do. When I arrived, the person at the desk asked me only one question: "Did you call the police, or did the police call you?" *Are you a perp or a victim?* was all they needed to know. I told her—*victim*—and she told them. And then I went into the room, in character, and the entire cast was there, in character, and we improvised a half-hour-long scene. It was a dream.

When they'd bring my character back for an episode, they would messenger me a script the day before the shoot. It's a union rule: these things need to go out the day before, so that everyone knows what to do. Down the left hand of the page were the technical specs: what kinds of lights they'd need and how many of what kind of cameras. And then down the right, the dialogue. Which in the case of *Reno 911!* would be, in full: "They have dinner," or "They talk." And that's it. And then I'd show up on camera, and before we'd shoot they ask me to *try* not to laugh, but if I had to, to try to hold it for one second so that the editor could piece a scene together. And I would mostly fail and so would everybody else, because these were the funniest people on the planet, working their hardest, together.

✦ ✦ ✦

It doesn't always go like that.

A couple years later, I got another one of those calls from my manager: *The daytime department from [major network] wants to see you. Go!* I knew going in was that it was a pilot for a daily talk show with "a name" and a cohost role that had not yet been filled. Great. I like to talk. Bring it on.

A young woman from the development department met me in reception and took me down to a conference room where I'd be meeting with her and her boss. On the way down the endless hallway, she—let's call her Madison—asked what I knew about the project. I said I knew pretty much nothing. She said: "Oh! Well, it's a daily, *Regis & Kelly* kind of a talk show, except it'll be Tori Spelling and a gay guy."

Pardon me?

"Tori loves her gays. Do you know her?"

I do not know Tori, and Tori does not know me, but I am gay, therefore Tori loves me. And in order to replicate the success of Regis Philbin and Kelly Ripa's time-tested chemistry, the network was going to pair Tori Spelling with Some Gay Guy. Oh, brother. I felt my pulse quickening. This was not going to go well.

Because here's what I hear when someone says they *love their gays:* I hear that they love the animated gay stylists they see on TV. I hear that they love someone who is ready with a quip and a snap and a *Hey, girlfriend, why are you crying and eating Wheat Thins?* I hear they love a mascot in a vest and a bow tie who can put them in a daring up-do and then go away quietly. I hear *I love my eunuchs.* I hate it.

So I met Madison's boss—whom we will call McKenzie— and we sat down and made chitchat for a moment. I knew instantly I was not going to get this job because they had really tucked themselves in for a bottomless pitcher of pizzazz, and I was absolutely not the man to serve it to them. They looked down at their clipboard of fun party questions:

"What do you and your girlfriends like to talk about?" Oh, boy.

"Um, I guess . . . when I am talking to my female friends . . . we talk about . . . what we are doing at the time?" No sale.

"What's, like, a dream weekend with your girlfriends?" Christ Almighty.

"I don't know. New Orleans Jazzfest?" Their eyes glazed over.

Finally McKenzie, desperate for any glimmer of glitter, said, "Let's talk relationships. My gays"—again with *my gays*—"give me the *best* relationship advice. What kind of relationship advice do you give your girlfriends?"

And I could hold it in any longer. I said: "Do any of your gays tell you that you should spend more time among heterosexual men?"

"What do you mean?"

"Like, do they tell you to hang out with men who can *love you back*? Because if they don't, they are not giving you good advice. They might be giving you *funny* advice, or *advice that rhymes*, but they are not giving you good advice."

McKenzie nodded, looked back at her clipboard, and said "Ouch." No fucking kidding ouch.

Madison stepped up: "Like, do you do any GAY things?"

I said, "Yeah, I do the two or three important ones," and they both sat up and asked what those were, and I chose not to explain the joke.

The worst part was looking at them and knowing they were kind people who were trying their best.

And listen: In my life, I have been told that as I gay man I am a threat to the American family. I have been told that to accept me as an equal is an insult to God. I have been told that I am no better than a pedophile. I have been told that I cannot serve in the military because my presence will undermine unit cohesion. I have had bottles thrown at me when I gathered with others to protest for marriage equality. I have been told that I am sick, that I am damaged, and that I am damage and sickness incarnate.

Let the record show that what finally made me snap is the suggestion that I was supposed to have chemistry with Tori Spelling.

It didn't stop there. In the post–*The View* glut of panel

shows, I went in for chemistry test after chemistry test. I would always *almost* book the job, and then at the last minute not book the job, and it was always because—this is a thing I have been told more than once to my face—"For the gay guy slot, we need a *really* gay guy." Which it was explained to me—and honestly, you haven't lived until you've had someone explain how people like you are supposed to behave—meant: quips and zingers, a lot of fashion talk, constant sexual innuendo. Where a few years before, anti-gay propaganda would have led to my losing a job, I was suddenly losing jobs for not behaving enough like anti-gay propaganda.

And I was starting to fall out of love with television.

19

Trying to Find a Balance

IF IT IS UNCOMFORTABLE BEING A FAT GUY IN A GAY bar, it is straight-up agony being overweight in Los Angeles. You are surrounded on all sides by healthy, glowing individuals with jobs they don't really need to go to every day, and every day is cloudless and 72 degrees, inviting them out of their homes to run, hike, bike, or otherwise show their bodies off.

Previously, I had been a fairly active person. I went to the gym. I rollerbladed. I ran until I couldn't run anymore, which generally meant about a mile and a quarter. And then I drank fifteen draft beers out of filthy taps, ate pizza at three in the morning, soaked up my hangovers with Sausage McGriddles, and had the nerve to wonder why I was fat and tired.

But in Los Angeles, I adopted healthy habits one at a time. I bought a bike and I started waking up an hour earlier in the morning to ride it. I started going to bed at grown-up times, which is easy because the bars close at 2:00 a.m. and are filled with people who moved to town to be on *Big Brother*. I started feeling stronger, more energetic.

Except each morning I woke up feeling like a medium-sized human being was sitting on my chest, and it took me longer than I'm comfortable admitting to connect it to the fact that I still smoked. So I quit, by which I mean that I told everyone I didn't smoke anymore but barely altered my habits one bit. On a visit west, my old roommate Lee asked: "If you don't smoke anymore, why is it that you still smoke?" I said: "Oh, it's hard. Maybe I'll get hypnotized or do Chantix or something." "Oh," he said, "I have an idea for you." And then he leaned in close and looked me right in the eye. "Have you tried *being a man?*"

I nodded and stubbed out my cigarette, and I have not had once since. As Catholic priests, nuns, and educators have known for centuries, shame is a powerful deterrent.

If you drop a habit, you want to pick one up. What I decided to do was train for a triathlon. Southern California has the benefit of year-round perfect weather, so there is always a race to train for. I chose Wildflower, up in San Luis Obispo, because it has the reputation of being the hardest in the country, and I am an idiot. I bought myself a wetsuit, joined a training team to raise money for cancer, and started bragging about it immediately.

The first training swim was in a high-school pool out in the Valley, and we were directed to show up with a swim cap and a pair of goggles, neither of which I brought. My coach said, "No goggles?" I said, "Yeah, no, sorry, forgot." He said, "*Chlorine*, though." I said, "Yeah, I'll be fine." I'd been in pools; I knew chlorine.

I did not know chlorine. What I knew was my parents' pool, which contained a moderate amount of chlorine. I had not experienced a *high-school* pool, whose chlorine levels had to combat teenage acne, athlete's foot, staph infections, and whatever venereal diseases kids are passing around these days. This pool was *all* chlorine, and my eyes were completely unprotected.

I didn't notice how badly I'd injured myself until after it was over. In the showers, my eyes began to sting, and then to burn, and then to sting and burn so intensely that I began looking for an emergency eyewash station, which I couldn't find because I wasn't in an industrial chemistry lab and also I couldn't see. And then the tears came, in furious rivers, doing their healing work. Soon, the pain subsided. And then ten minutes later, when I was in my car heading out of the place, it started again. I pulled over and cried medicinal tears into an old T-shirt out of my gym bag. It passed again. And then it kept coming again, and again, in waves that increased in intensity, every ten minutes or so. Pain, tears, relief.

My improv team King Ten had a show that night, and I had about an hour to eat dinner before I had to be at the theater. So I found myself a Rockin' Sushi place on Ventura, where I could sit at the bar and have a protein-rich meal in at least partial darkness. I took a seat, ordered a few pieces, and then the process started again. Stinging eye heat, and then a soothing deluge of tears.

What I'm saying is that I was sitting by myself at a popular sushi bar, crying.

Do you remember when I told you that I will be recognized only at times when I am not at my best? Sitting at a sushi bar, in the middle of their dinner rush, alone, sobbing uncontrollably, was one of those times. In between tear waves, I heard someone at a nearby table say, "Hey, isn't that that guy from MTV up at the bar?" And their friend said, "Yeah. Don't say anything, though. I think he's having a rough night." And then I cried even harder.

My strategy at any sushi bar is to begin and end with toro. It's the star of the show, fish-wise, so it's good to kick off a meal with it, and then to let it be your grand finale. As the sushi chef handed over my last piece of toro, I couldn't pull the plate away, because he was holding on to it. He was trying to get my attention, and this was the only way he knew how. We were both holding on to that final plate, and I looked up at him and his gaze met my tear-stained eyes. He looked at me with real, honest compassion, and said to me: "Me too sometimes."

I wept the real way when I crossed the finish line of the triathlon. I did three more that year, and made them a permanent part of my life. I started doing the Malibu Celebrity Triathlon every year, because their definition of "celebrity" was broad, and the year Jennifer Lopez did it, we finished the swim at around the same time. If you got *US Weekly* the next week, you saw a picture of her in the celebrity transition area, changing flawlessly from her swimwear to her bike gear, and you also saw me just behind her, grimacing and pink, struggling out of my wetsuit.

So then I entered the lottery for the New York Marathon, and unfortunately I got into the New York Marathon. I lost whole weekends of my life doing eighteen-mile training runs. I lost toenails. But I did not lose weight; my race pictures show me in a skin-tight running shirt that hugs my massive belly. Even the ultimate endurance event—the race whose first participant finished it and then *died*—couldn't move the needle.

I was a fat endurance athlete. I still ate like an unsupervised teenager through this whole time in my life and failed to see the connection.

At around this time in California, I started to notice friends of mine getting involved in a thing called Crossfit. It seemed to follow the same pattern: one by one they would:

- get into it,
- start looking terrific,
- begin to talk to one another about it,
- never stop talking to one another about it,
- never stop talking to *me* about it, and then
- injure a knee or a shoulder and have to stop.

I thought: *If it causes actual physical harm and turns its users into willing zombies, it must be great. This might be for me.* It's a mind-set similar to what draws less-cautious people to heroin.

So I went. A Crossfit gym—they are called "boxes" officially, but continuing to call them "gyms" is how I convince myself that I am *in* but not *of* this world—opened up near me, and I figured that a new place would have a higher concentration of beginners—and perhaps a lower percentage of loud people with perfect bodies—so I joined.

I hated it from the moment I walked in the door and I've been back five times a week ever since.

Here's the deal: Crossfit is full of peacocky guys whose shirts come off the second the workout begins, to the point where you think: *If this is how you're going to be, why wear a shirt at all, anywhere?* It is full of personal-trainer-looking women who will critique your push-up form, even if they're not your actual personal trainer. You will work out to the point of intense and violent vomit, and you will come very close to getting in your car and going home. You will learn a thing called a "burpee," which requires you to flop onto the ground, peel yourself back up onto your heels, jump up in the air and clap, and then do that a bunch of times in a row. You will be surrounded by people who talk about Crossfit and nothing else, who tell Crossfit jokes and wear Crossfit shirts that say things like "Buck Furpees." You will do all this while you listen to Rage Against The Machine. It is deeply unpleasant.

It also works. If you're diligent, after a few weeks of burpees and Olympic weightlifting moves, and the meat-intensive Paleo diet, you will notice a change in your body. You will see muscles you have never seen. (And also you will feel them, and they will feel sore.) You will have to buy new, smaller pants. People will ask you what you've been doing, and then you will watch the regret wash over their faces when you talk about Crossfit for an hour. You may injure yourself severely or have a meat-induced heart attack before you're fifty, but you will have had abs for a moment before you go, and it will have been worth it.

I was pulling it together physically, but my mind was still a mess. I was still drinking like a college kid, still throwing myself at the wrong guys, still generally behaving like the scrub TLC wanted none of.

Right around the time I started Crossfit, I did a shoot at a house on the Pacific Coast Highway in Malibu. A lot of people who have houses right there on the beach rent them out as filming locations, because how else are you going to make a mortgage payment like that? This place was a smallish shack in a little private surfing cove—a place where Big Kahuna would live in one of those Frankie and Annette movies. Along one wall there were acoustic guitars. Along another: surfboards. And along a third: psychology textbooks. I was intrigued, doubly so when I met the owner of the house, who was among the most attractive men I'd ever seen in person. So I had to ask, because I was fascinated and also because I wanted more reasons to stand near him: "What's the deal with all the psychology books?" He said, "I just got my degree and my license to work as a clinical psychologist, and I'm going to run my practice out of my home. Instead of sitting in an office talking for an hour, we'll grab surfboards and paddle out past the breakers to where it's nice and still, and we'll do our sessions out there in the ocean."

I said, "Do you take Blue Cross?" He did not. I made an appointment anyway and have gone every other week since. And every other week, after I have finished a session talking about my feelings with my hot therapist in the Pacific Ocean, I think: "This is so absurdly Southern California that every single person I grew up with would never stop laughing if they knew about it."

Good. Let them.

In Which I Meet My Dream Man

AFTER SHANE, I dated a long list of Los Angeles archetypes: The guy who got his dog high. The bartender who always seemed to have a little too much energy, and then I found out he sprinkled meth in his own drinks, like some kind of evil Crystal Light. The namedropper, who mentioned five hundred times over the course of one lunch that he's college friends with Leigh Nash, the lead singer of Sixpence None The Richer. (When I didn't call this guy back, he sent me an e-mail: "Listen, I guess we weren't a match, but can you do me a favor? Can you tell me what you thought of me? Just a few sentences, a paragraph or two, about how I looked and what my conversation was like and what you thought was good and what you thought was bad? I keep asking my friends and they won't tell me!!! So if you could do that by the end of this week, I'd really appreciate it." Like I'm Yelp. No, thanks.)

Then one night, the perfect man walked into my life.

I was on a weekend getaway in San Diego with my friends Heith and Nathan, and we'd been hitting all the Hillcrest hotspots. On Saturday nights, starting at 9:30 p.m.—and not one moment before; gay social life in San Diego follows a rigorous schedule—the action was at Hamburger Mary's, a burger place at the top of Hillcrest. There's a smallish dance floor in the main room there, and on the far side of it, a slim doorway into another room with a similarly sized dance floor. Both rooms were packed, because we showed up at 10 p.m., fashionably late. It was '90s Nostalgia Night, which was alarming, and as Robyn's "Do You Know What It Takes" started pumping out of the speakers, I grabbed my boys and we hit the floor. This was my jam.

By this time, I'd learned to mistrust the entire idea of dating in Southern California. The boys are too pretty and too looks-conscious. Too connected and too status-obsessed. A bunch of beautiful men looking for their identical twin. I had resigned myself to the fact that I wasn't going to meet a man at this place, partially because I meant it and partially because everyone tells you you meet your soulmate when you stop looking. But then, of course, the second you stop looking, you start thinking *Is this it? Is this when it's going to happen, now that I'm not looking?*, which is its own insidious way of still looking. It's a vicious cycle. Fuck it; I was there to dance.

And then I saw him.

He was on the dance floor in the next room, throwing down some heat. He was a little heavy, but his hair was perfect. He was in a tweed sportcoat, just like I was. (Tweed? In San Diego? Who does that? Besides this guy and me?) We locked eyes for a split-second and then I looked away. *Don't stare, Dave. You're going to have to play this one just right.* I got back to dancing, fixating on this guy and all the things we'd have to talk about. *You sometimes feel out of place in this silly, shallow place too? You feel pre-judged, and you overdress? Pretty Tweed Guy: are you lonely, just like me?*

I tried not to look over, but I couldn't help myself. Each time I did, though, it seemed his eyes were right on mine. Locked, like Maverick's missile system in *Top Gun*. (Top Gun *is pivotal for him, too,* I thought.) I immediately looked away so as not to be caught staring, and then I caught another glance, and then another, and then another. He did the same. *Oh, it is on. It's on like B. D. Wong.*

I decided to go say hello. "Gotta go see about a boy," I told my friends, and took a few steps toward the adjoining room. I looked through the crowd to see if he was still there, and he was. He was walking my way. *Yes.* I was too self-conscious to look him in the eye, but his jacket was exquisite: a tiny bit frayed at the button holes, just the way I liked. We took a few more steps toward one another until we were nearly face-to-face. My breath was getting short.

And then I chickened out. *I can't do this. I'm coming in way too hot here. I'm going to give this another pass. I'll scooch right by him, give him a good look in the face, nod hello, and then go get another whiskey and stare at him for another twenty minutes.* We approached the narrow portal between the two dance floors. I juked left, to get around him.

So did he. I faked right. So did he.

It was one of those things like you do on the sidewalk or in the hallway at work, where you're each trying to get out of the other's way but you keep getting right in each other's way, and then one of you says "shall we dance," except in this case we were *actually dancing.*

I was about to have a meet-cute on a dance floor in a gay club and I was powerless to stop it.

We moved closer.

Closer.

Right. *Wait, I think I actually own that shirt!*

Closer.

Left. Is he . . . smiling?

Closer.

Closer.

"Hi."

SMACK.

I stepped back and I was dazed for a moment before I realized that two friends of mine and a packed dance floor full of gay people had just watched as I walked right into a floor-to-ceiling mirror.

From there, I decided to start talking to guys in bars more, especially once I had confirmed that they were not actually me. *I'm not getting any younger*, I thought, *I have learned through substantial experience how to handle rejection, I should just go for it and say hi to people.* So I said "Hi" to guys and sometimes it worked and sometimes it didn't, but it felt good to try. A month or two later, I was at the Otherroom on Abbot Kinney for my birthday, and I went up to the bar to get a round of drinks. Beside me, there was a youngish blond guy who was handsome but didn't seem to be even the tiniest bit aware of it, which made him that much more so. I said "Hi," he said "Hi," we made chit-hat. I asked him to come sit at our table, and he did, and his name was Ben. He was a composer, and my friends seemed to like him.

The topic of conversation was the new *Rock Star: INXS* show CBS was about to launch—a singing competition where the remaining members of the band would try to find a new Michael Hutchence. Specifically, the topic of conversation was what they'd say each week when a contestant got cut. There were a million of these competitive reality shows that year, and each one came with a snappy little elimination line, like Martha Stewart saying "You're not on the list" in hers, or Heidi Klum telling the losers on Project Runway "You're out." It had to be pithy; it had to have something to do with the subject matter; and it had to look good on a T-shirt or a mug. We all threw out our suggestions: "We don't need you tonight?" "You are not the one thing?" "*Do* change?" This is the kind of thing improv people like to do, because it involves quick thinking and making jokes and showing off. And then Ben, who was not an improv guy, said: "Oh, I've got it." And we all looked at him.

"You choked."

He's been around ever since.

20

Losing My Edge

HEN YOU'RE YOUNG, YOU THINK YOU'RE ALWAYS going to know every song in the Top 40. You feel pity for the old people who have to ask you what's playing on the radio. If you think about their tastes at all, you assume they've always been this out of touch. Incapable of keeping up since forever. Old even when they were young.

And then one day it happens to you.

One afternoon in late 2001, when I was back in New York for a visit, I was walking east on Seventh Street with one of my old neighbors. A few yards in front of us, five young guys were walking west. They had greasy hair mussed just so, little tiny denim or leather jackets, filthy Chuck Taylors—the neighborhood uniform. They were beautiful, even the one who looked a little like Paula Poundstone. They frightened me, not because I was afraid they'd beat me up, but because they reminded me of my mortality.

My neighbor made what I would call a muffled beeping sound, and then they passed and he exhaled sharply and whispered in my ear: "Did you see who that was?" I said I didn't. He grabbed at his chest and shot me a gaze of disbelief. "Dave. That was The Strokes." He turned around. "That. Was. The Strokes," and then, suddenly bold, he just shouted it out:

"FABRIIIIIZIOOOOO!" One of them, Fabrizio I guess, pumped a fist into the air.

Huh. That was the who now?

I looked at pictures back at his place, and his story checked out. That was The Strokes, all five of them, out catting around together in the final moments before they could cat around without security. The Strokes were who the people with their ears to the ground were listening to and talking about at the moment, and while I guess I had heard the name, I hadn't listened to or talked about them. He burned me a copy of *Is This It* and I devoured it that very day, mostly out of shame for not having done it already. I loved it immediately, because it is great, but also because I felt like it was my duty to love it. To have missed the new hot thing was bad enough; to miss it, listen to it, and not get it would have been too much to bear. I'd be buying those Rod Stewart *Great American Songbook* compilations from Starbucks by the end of the week if I wasn't careful.

The Strokes were the first band to whiz right past me. They had become the biggest thing going, and nobody had bothered to check with me first. It hurt.

They broke down a door, and the kids streamed through it in the months that followed: new bands with creative dress codes and names you couldn't believe hadn't been taken yet: The Hives. The Vines. The Killers. The White Stripes. The Black Keys. Jet, for fuck's sake. There was a rock resurgence, and its sound was inspired by all sorts of things I liked, and then I actually looked at the bands and I realized: *Oh, dear God, I am much older than these people. I have as many years on these people as my brothers have on me.*

This was the new generation. And I was not in it.

Back in Los Angeles, The Strokes did one of those $2 Bill shows for MTV2, and I was still connected enough at the network to finagle a couple of seats. My friend Brian and I sat in the back, and during "Take It or Leave It," Julian left the stage and climbed over the crowd, all the way up to our row. A newly minted rock god, standing right in front of me. I stretched out my arms and he grabbed my shoulders, climbed up, and stood right on my lap. It's on YouTube; if you look closely, you can see me wondering what to do. I had the frontman of the biggest, coolest indie band in the country standing right on my thighs, and all I could do was wonder: *Is this the way the kids show disrespect? Is this his way of singling me out? Or is he just drunk?* That's another thing that happens when you age: you can no longer tell when young people are making fun of you.

It can't be helped. It's a sense that recedes over time, like all your senses do. I held on longer than most, because it was in my job description for a while, but the reaper comes for everyone. I still looked at *Billboard* every week, but more and more it felt like an eye chart, and I was quickly losing my vision. First there was a number one single I had never heard ("Bump Bump Bump" by B2K, sometime in 2003; I still don't know what it is, but I remember it well). Then I had never heard *anything* in the top ten, and just as quickly I had never heard *of* anything in the top ten. I saw a trailer for *Save the Last Dance* and thought "Right, like anyone will pay money to see that," and it made $30 million in its opening weekend. It hit me: pop culture can produce content without me or my peers in mind, and yet still be very successful.

It's like an insult from a good friend.

This all happens very quickly, and it doesn't unhappen. You won't age into someone else's prized demographic. (Actually, you will: Fox News'. Best not to think about it.)

Most people take this in stride. I did not. My entire identity revolved around being on top of pop culture. I had always prided myself on being a step ahead of what people were listening to. It was my superpower, and age was my Kryptonite, and my proof that I lost the battle is that I'm using a Superman reference here instead of a much more *au courant* Captain Marvel one.

If I don't know what's going on in the world of pop culture, *who am I?*

Now, of course there had always been bands of and for older people, but there was usually something a little embarrassing about them. They were always trying just a bit too hard. I think of the revolving coat rack covered in silk scarves that is Steven Tyler. I think of Mike Love and his repulsive Hawaiian shirts, mugging and pointing through another chorus of "Barbara Ann." God help me, I think of Cher. (I know, I know, but go see her the next time she mounts a farewell tour; it's ninety minutes of children dancing around her while she changes clothes twenty-seven times and gay men in velvet jackets rejoice.)

Is this what's waiting for me?

It's easier to get old and out of touch in Los Angeles, because in Los Angeles you don't have to see young people if you don't want to. You don't have to see *any* people. You can hang out in your house and your car and be exactly as social as you want to be. In the early '00s, satellite radio became a thing, and allowed you to listen only to what you already knew you liked. You could try the pop channel for a while, and then when the sound of being hit about the face with a pillowcase full of silverware got tiresome, you could turn it right to '80s on 8, and leave it there. You could hear "Walking on Sunshine" again, and it wouldn't remind you of eighth grade anymore, it would remind you of when you were stuck in traffic on Tuesday. Or you could cut out the middleman entirely, put your iPod on shuffle, and be your own radio station. It's not what you want for yourself, but it's comfortable. You can just stop growing and get old and die there in your car and nobody needs to know about it.

I was ready to do that.

I credit Craig Finn with saving my life.

The first Hold Steady song I ever heard was "Stevie Nix" from *Separation Sunday,* on one of the alternative stations. About a minute in, I pulled over my car and turned it up. It was a glorious mess of bar-band noise and *those lyrics.* Craig was less a singer at the time than a shouter, and what he shouted could just as well have been notes for a short story: vivid little vignettes about young drunks at rock shows and in ERs. A woman either getting clean or dying at age thirty-three, like Jesus. He wove in old punk bands, Catholic imagery, Fleetwood Mac, Mary Tyler Moore, and Rod Stewart. It was love.

They were playing at the Knitting Factory in a couple of weeks, and I scooped up tickets immediately. And when they took the stage, I had never felt more relieved in my life. *They were my age.* Praise Jesus, my new favorite band was my own age. So was the crowd: a bunch of weirdos who liked to read books, or who had had Catholic educations, or who just liked to get drunk at rock shows, or all three. The youth are always a minority at Hold Steady shows. We old people run things there.

I did my research on the band, and it turns out Craig Finn went to Boston College, class of 1993. My year. If I'd gone to the school that wanted me instead of begging my way into the one that didn't, the lead singer of my new favorite band might have been my roommate. (Amy Poehler would have been in our class too. God help us all.)

Cool grown-up bands appeared or reformed in the years after. The National. LCD Soundsystem. Superchunk got back together. So did Sleater-Kinney. And not for embarrassing reunion tours, like Foreigner or REO Speedwagon or whatever sad-sack old journeymen play the state fair circuit; they got back together and made vital music and rocked the fuck out on stage in their forties, like it was a thing you could do.

It didn't make me feel young—nothing can do that anymore—but it reconnected me to what made my youth exciting.

And then, in 2015, the Replacements got back together. Even when the Replacements—I am not going to call them the 'Mats, and neither should you; it is the indie rock version of mentioning your friend *Bobby De Niro,* and it should be avoided—were together, you never knew how together they were. They were liable to pass out on stage, or vomit, or fight, or break up. The records were great and have stood the test of time. The live shows were performance art.

When the tour dates were announced, every comedy writer in his or her (okay, almost exclusively *his*) forties took to Twitter to see who else was going, and in how many cities. All of us who'd been faving one another's tweets and helping to promote one another's shows made plans to actually meet in person.

And then they took the stage and they seemed to be sober,

and the songs sounded a little like they did on the records. They were actually *tight,* and everyone knew every word, and we all shouted along to "I Will Dare," a few thousand people whose love of the Replacements sent them on some kind of weird journey that landed them in Los Angeles.

My only complaint with the show was that they didn't bring up the lights and break us into small discussion groups.

In the twenty-first century, there are bands of people in their forties who are making music that makes my heart swell like it did when I was a teenager.

Someday I'm going to have to accept the fact that I'm old, but it doesn't have to be today.

21

I Wanna Get Better

A YEAR OR SO AGO, I WAS HIKING WITH MY FRIEND
David, and he asked me: "Hey, do you want to do a Peruvian cactus hallucinogen with a shamaness and explore your
emotions with a bunch of people in Topanga Canyon?" and
without hesitation, I said: "Absolutely." I mean, offers like this
come around rarely, even in Southern California. You have to
seize them. "That is absolutely something I want to do. Why
are we still talking about it instead of doing it?"

I had been in therapy for a couple of years by this time, and
I was learning plenty about myself and my hangups and the
things I'd need to get past if I want to move forward in this
life, but the thing about therapy is that it's very slow. You have
to talk, you have to listen, you have to make your progress in
tiny little baby steps. I don't have time for that. I am a busy
man. I need something that's going to whiz me right past all of
that sharing and learning and shit. A front-of-the-line pass to
enlightenment. Yes. I'm in.

I said yes to adventure, and then almost immediately I
started trying to figure out how to get out of it.

David added me to the e-mail list for the event. To this day,
I have no idea how *he* got on it, because it is best not to ask
questions in these situations; all roads lead to sketchtown. I

learned that the ceremony would be led by a South African shamaness named Pam, who traveled the world unblocking people's emotions, leading whole tour groups of people deep into the wilderness of their own souls. It seemed more responsible, more noble and mature than my youthful drug experiences. It felt like *homework*. The hallucinogen of choice was a substance called San Pedro, created from the pulverized innards of Peruvian cacti and consumed as a tea. According to Shamaness Pam's website, San Pedro is known as the spirit of St. Peter, a masculine, guiding spirit that takes you deep into your mind, your soul, your past, your problems, and whispers your solutions to you, like your big brother would. (Of course, anyone who has ever had an older brother knows that whispering your problems and solutions to you is not part of that particular package, but I was eager to believe.) The cancellation policy on a thing like this turns out to be lenient, because what is a shamaness going to do if you flake on her jungle drug group therapy expedition, take you to court? I signed up, and then the morning came along and I chickened out. Someone else went in my place and everyone had terrific insights and a wonderful, serene journey, and I immediately felt like an asshole for having bailed. I apologized to Pam via text and made a plan to do it the next time she brought her soul circus to town.

Shamaness Pam made a return visit about six months later, and since I was still on the e-mail list, I got an early alert. A woman named Sarabeth, whose name on her e-mail account was "sarabliss," alerted me to the new event. "Beautiful soul: I am excited and lucky to tell you about a sacred healing ceremony in . . ." and I stopped reading. I said: "Holmes, you are not going to bail on this." I reserved a spot, and then immediately calling and texting friends, begging them to come along.

12

David had already learned plenty about his soul; Ben seemed halfway on board; and my friend Matt gave a tentative yes.

You were supposed to bring a check with you, and you were not supposed to write anything in the memo line about what the check is actually for. I loved this detail, because it meant that at least once, someone had written "HEALING JUNGLE HALLUCINOGEN CEREMONY" or "SACRED TRIPOUT," or simply "DRUGS." The whole thing would cost $250, inclusive of a vegan comedown meal in the early evening and all the organic mango you could handle, all day long. I circled the date on my calendar, and I promised to stick to it this time.

The morning of the ceremony, Ben and Matt cancelled on me, which I chalked up to karma, because I was already talking like a poorly written acid-victim character from an '80s movie, and I went ahead anyway.

The event was to take place in the Laurel Canyon home and grounds of someone very wealthy and trusting. I got in my car, took a few deep, calming breaths, and drove up there. Along the snaking, endless driveway was foreign SUV after foreign SUV, with California, Arizona, and Nevada plates— the footprint of Southwestern hippies who don't care about their carbon footprint. The men getting out of their cars wore long, flowing Maharishi shirts and Tom's Shoes. The women wore Lululemon yoga pants and espadrilles, and most of them were being played by Molly Shannon. Everyone seemed to know one another.

When I walked through the open front door of this Laurel Canyon palace, the song playing on the expensive and ear-splitting sound system was "Proud," by Heather Small, which you may know as the theme song from NBC's *The Biggest*

Loser. Echoing off the tiled walls was "ah-*WHAT* HAVE YA *DONE* TA-*DAY* TA *MAKE* YA *FEEEEEL* PROUD."

I shook the hands of a few gentlemen in billowing linen, and then I was hugged from behind by a stranger. "Hello, beloved," a complete stranger said, "I'm Butterbean." *Of course you are,* I thought. *Get your hands off me.*

Shamaness Pam was ninety minutes late, so we all spent a lot of time wandering the grounds, checking out the giant house and the huge pool and the grotto. The house was *massive.* As the people around me cooed about how blessed we were to be in this home, all I could think was: How do you get this rich and still have time to hallucinate? The man of the house, Rafael, offered no hints. The really wealthy ones never do. He and his eighteen-year-old son would be tripping with us, and his new wife would be there with their *maybe* one-month-old child, sober and supervising. Still, a couple dozen strangers hallucinating around an infant. Yikes.

When Shamaness Pam showed up, she got her cactus trip-out tea party show on the road lickety-split. What we would do was this: we'd go around the circle, one by one, each of us holding a glass of water, into which Shamaness Pam would dump one large spoonful of dark green powder. We'd stir and drink quickly and then be given an organic lollipop in the flavor of our choosing: yellow or green. (I went yellow.) There were about twenty-five of us, so the circle was big and the process took a good half-hour. The perimeter was studded with Moroccan pillows and small trash cans lined with plastic bags in case anyone needed to barf. A lot of people needed to barf. We were, after all, drinking poison.

Afterward, we were to go around the same circle and state our intention for the day. As you have probably already guessed, there was a "talking stick," which we would pass from person to person, and only the one holding it would be allowed to speak. I was near the top of the circle, because I wanted to get all of this over with, so I got my intentions out of the way early. I was quick and direct: "I feel like there's something I need to get off my chest, something I need to discover, or examine, or something, and I'm hoping this can loosen me up enough so that I can find it. So. Um. Namaste?" I spat this out in about two seconds, because I was nervous, and I didn't want this mystery cactus drug to kick in while I was in the middle of a sentence, or worse, listening to rich hippies talk. "Namaste," the circle answered.

As the talking stick passed from person to person, the stories got longer and longer, because if there's one thing people who have the time and money to take a day off and explore their souls enjoy more than expensive sandals, it's the sound of their own voice. *Oh, you're going to talk about finding your quiet inner voice? Well then I'm going to chant my intention.* It was a goddamn bliss-off. About halfway through the circle, people just started taking the stick, breathing huge, showy cleansing breaths and saying "Wow," and then pausing for fifteen seconds before launching into a monologue of jumbled Oprah words. It went on for a good hour. (It was actually not a very good hour.)

Finally the last person stated his intention—which was the same as everyone else's and either took ten minutes or my dose was starting to kick in and my perception of time was warping—and we were dismissed to spend the rest of the day plunging the depths of our soul wherever we chose. I sprinted outside to find a good seat by the pool. I shook off the stress of the yoga-people talk, breathed deeply, and began to focus on the questions that led me here. What is it about me that has me perpetually on the outside? Why can't I just relax? *Who am I, anyway?*

Just then, an older guy in a long white T-shirt and linen pants walked up behind me, gave me a rough and unbidden scalp massage and whispered into my ear: "I can't wait to connect with *youuuuuu.*"

Oh, *no.*

I said, "Oh! Oh, my gosh, thanks! Me, too," and he loped up a rock wall behind me, like some kind of mountain cat.

It wasn't until this point that I started looking around me at the rest of the tripping hippies on the grounds. I took a good look at them and noticed that about a quarter were vomiting, another quarter were growling and kicking like animals, and everyone else was either crying and writhing on the ground like slow-motion sea bass in a fishing boat or dancing to the beat of the drum one guy was playing (in a situation like this one guy is always going to be playing a drum). Shamaness Pam made an appearance outside to remind everyone that the owner of the house would prefer that we barfed at the base of the olive tree, to help fertilize it. Those who were vomiting heard her and nodded, and then they calmly walked or writhed their way to the olive tree to offer it their special gift.

I have always had what I believe is a healthy fear of hallucinogens, but this was fairly pleasant. Nothing major happened, no melting trees or devil faces. The walls pulsated slightly and the clouds gave me a mild kaleidoscope effect and that was about it. Decent. Manageable. I found a place on the grass to meditate, just as Shamaness Pam came outside to offer those who felt they needed it a second dose. I probably could have gone with a second dose. I felt in control, and I felt like if this thing was going to work, I might want to get a little *out* of control. I thought I might want to lose myself so that I could find myself again.

But then I realized that if I took a second helping, there was no way I'd be able to drive before the next morning, and I'd probably have to spend the night in a sleeping bag around these people in a situation that I was 94 percent sure was going to turn into an orgy. Unacceptable. A handful of people took her up on it, and I sat in the sun and counted my breaths, trying to quiet my mind and focus on the here and now.

And then all the people who took a second dose came back outside, sat right around me, breathed deeply, and barfed.

After a couple of hours, the guy who wanted to connect with me came and sat at my side, and I thought: *Okay, fine, let's do this. I mean, I'm here and the clouds are dancing, let's connect.* He began to breathe, slowly, loudly, and I began to breathe with him. Ahhhhh. OOOOOOHHH. Together. Breathing as one. It felt nice, actually. Just breathing, connecting, doing whatever it was that we were doing, in a place where everyone was too busy dancing or vomiting to judge. Powerful. Almost sexual.

He whispered into my ear: "You're intense." I agreed. "Do you know the circumstances of your birth?" I said I heard I was a c-section, but didn't have any clear memories. He said, "Well, it was traumatic. I know that. Your chi is blocked. Do you want me to call the healer over?" I said: "I mean, you probably should."

He went over to the healer, who was on the porch doing a bong hit, They had a conversation about me that I could not hear, but their body language was that of EMTs on the scene of a head-on car crash. My blocked chi was going to have to get fixed. Twenty CCs of bullshit juice, stat.

The healer came over to me and said: "I saw you when you stated your intention, and I've been wanting to get my hands on you ever since. Lay down." I laid down. Connection Guy said: "I'm going to hold space with you," and I said "Oh, thank you so much!" The healer shook a rattle around my body. She drank from a giant bottle that looked like where Barbara Eden lived in *I Dream of Jeannie* and spat what I am fairly certain was bay rum all over me. She whistled around my chakras, pausing at my navel to whisper, so quietly I could barely hear it, "come on, baby. Come on out. That's right. *That's good. That's right.*" And then the healing was over. The healer looked at me with a look of absolute triumph. "How's that?" I said: "Boy, you really did it. Thanks." She gave me her card—she's also a life coach and professional organizer—and I told her I'd call. I thanked Connection Guy. And then I slipped out the door when nobody was looking and sat in my car listening to music until the sky stopped breathing so I could drive home.

I put my iPhone on shuffle, and the drugs absolutely worked in that I felt each song deeply. Dawes's "A Little Bit of Everything" made me think about our interconnectedness and the fragility of life and the importance of hope. Mayer Hawthorne's "The Stars Are Ours" reminded me of my friends all over the country and how lucky I was to have them. The Hold Steady's "Our Whole Lives" got me thinking about Catholicism and how it shaped me, whether I continued to embrace it or not. And then I drove home and Ben asked me how it was and I told him we'd talk about it later, but right now let's make a YouTube playlist of all of Janet Jackson's videos, in order, and watch them on the big screen with our Apple TV. And he immediately said yes, because I am absolutely with the right guy.

The next day, I woke up early, with a fresh, clean mind and a newly cleansed chakra system. I had two unread e-mails, one from Shamaness Pam to the whole group with a photograph of some items that had been left at the house: a feather earring; a leather cuff; a colander; a small, fine-mesh satchel with a baby tooth inside. The other was from my friend John in Ireland, asking for a full rundown on how the whole thing went. I said: "I didn't get any answers. I didn't learn anything about myself. All I wanted was to get away from these people and be on my own and listen to music. I think I did it wrong."

And he hit me back immediately: "What if that's your answer?"

And I stood right up out of my chair.

What if that's my answer? What if I took a shaman-approved jungle hallucinogen that is supposed to give you insight into your soul, and my soul told me: "Rather than try to fit in somewhere that's not for you, you're better off on your own, wandering, writing, listening, observing?"

What if I've been trying to join teams and wear uniforms and live by other people's rules my whole life, when what I should have been doing is trusting myself, like The Indigo Girls told me over Singapore Slings at Applebee's?

What if I am my whole team, and what if I always will be, and what if that's enough?

What if the millennia-old soul of Saint Peter really was in that cactus, and the secret he had traveled through time and over dimensions to whisper into my ear was: *Do you?*

As sacred pseudo-religious epiphanies go, it was as good as any.

I choose to believe.

Bonus Track

WAS WORKING IN THE OFFICE AT *ESQUIRE* IN NEW YORK City on June 26, 2015, the day the Supreme Court issued their decision in *Obergefell v. Hodges* and made marriage equality the law in all fifty states. The decision came down in the morning, and we had to get the news out and write our instant takes and collect the best Twitter reactions, all the musts for a magazine these days. There was rejoicing, and because it was 2015, we expressed it by sending each other Chuck Norris GIFs in HipChat. (But we meant it. It was a great morning. Those Chucks had never been more sincere.)

Once we'd gotten all our content up, I made the decision to relive the '90s and make it a Summer Friday, like in my advertising days, and I CitiBiked down to the Stonewall Inn. It seemed right: the modern gay rights movement had started with a riot there forty-six years before, nearly to the day. Plus, Pride Weekend was about to start. Say what you will about the Supreme Court, but they really know how to create a moment.

Just about everybody in the media had had the same idea. There were cameras and crews from all the local stations, radio reporters roaming with microphones, photographers clicking away. Everyone looking for a quote, a face, a fist, the perfect picture. I was, too.

But the windows were rattling from the thumping bass inside, and this was too important a day just to stand and observe. So I went in.

It was shoulder-to-shoulder inside, and the music was louder than the speakers could handle. You couldn't hear anyone talk, which was okay because what was there to say? We'd won. We just looked at each other: couples, groups of friends, people like me who'd come alone just to be there. We looked at each other and smiled. People sang along—Calvin Harris had bumped Robin S. from the rotation since the last time I'd been in a New York City gay bar—and jumped up and down. We had all taken our own winding, treacherous path to that place on that day, but we'd all made it. A few decades ago we would have been thrown into paddy wagons just for being there, but as of that morning, we were a part of the American family.

My people.

I jumped up and down with them.

The ground shook.

It felt like a new beginning. And as we've learned, every new beginning comes from some other beginning's end.

+   +   +

I had to run up to Mamaroneck for a friend's engagement party that evening, and after I'd been there for a couple hours, my friend's nephew came up and introduced himself. "I'm Justin," he said, a jubilant, braced-and-pompadoured kid fit for YouTube. "I heard you were coming. Have you had any of the seven-layer dip? That was me." We chatted for a good long time, me and Justin; he was twelve, about to start eighth grade at the local Catholic school. "Ooh, junior high," I said. "That was a rough one on me. How do you like it?"

"Are you kidding? I love it."

I said: "That was the age we all started going to mixers. Are there still mixers?" He said there were. Because I honestly had no idea of the answer to this question, I asked: "What do they play at a mixer these days?"

"Hip-hop, mostly. But, like, the hard stuff. Big Sean." And then he leaned in and stage-whispered, *"the clean versions."* Just a hint of an eye roll.

"When I was your age," I told him, "we wouldn't actually *mix* for about the first hour. The boys would be on one side, the girls on the other, and then someone would finally go out into the middle and dance and everyone would follow."

"Oh, we dance," he assured me. "Me and my friends? *We dance.*" I believed him.

I had met Justin's dad earlier in the night, and I saw him looking over at the two of us talking, and I may have been imagining it, but I thought I saw a look of *okay, good* on his face. I got the feeling we were supposed to be talking, Justin and I.

Now, maybe young Justin is a gay kid, like I suspect he is. Maybe he's not. What he definitely is is an exuberant twelve-year-old boy who will never spend five minutes of his one life thinking he shouldn't be.

I like that I grew up uncomfortable. It gave me the fuel that powered me through a very weird life. It made me want to succeed, it made me want to work hard, and it got me where I always wanted to be. But it's not for everyone.

Maybe Justin will have his first crush and be able to tell his friends and parents about it. Maybe Justin will make an ass of himself falling in colossal stupid love with someone when he's fourteen, when you're supposed to make your embarrassing mistakes, and he'll get to shake it off, the way everyone else does. Maybe Justin will stay this confident and composed throughout his youth, and when he's my age, all he'll be able to say is that his life is pretty plain. What a luxury.

He's part of the family now, and while being in the family is no guarantee he'll be treated well, it does mean he'll be treated like everyone else.

I wish Justin the very best, and I believe he's going to get the very best, and I have to believe it because it would be unseemly for me to follow him on Instagram and make sure.

All I can say is that I think we're both lucky guys.

ACKNOWLEDGMENTS

TO EVERYONE IN THE INSANE CROWN POSSE, PARTICU-larly my brilliant, patient, and perceptive editor, Matt Inman. You are the best, and I am the luckiest. To my agent, Michael Bourret, for believing I had something to say, and to Michele Rubin for being the first to make me think I could do this. To John Sellers for all of the encouragement. To Joe Armenia, Caryn Leigh Posnansky, Veronica Robledo, Rod Aissa, David Katz, Amanda Schatz Kitaeff, Dave Strevens, and literally everyone at MTV. To all at *Esquire*, *Vulture*, and SiriusXM. To Grant Goodeve. To Steph Edwards, Katie Reap, Sarah Brick, Teddy Harris, the day shift at Longman & Eagle, and the entire city of Chicago. To everybody at iO West, NerdMelt, and *Maximum Fun*. To Andrew Lear. To Fr. Ralph. To Josh & Shell, Scott & Jules, Derek & Debbie, Dave, Matt, Irene, Crowley, Nick & Elise, Mike & Allison, Lee & Hannah, John & Hank, everyone whose name I mentioned in this book, and all of my friends on both coasts and everywhere in between. To the cast of *The Friday Forty*. To Jensen Karp for being an ear and a shoulder. To Kara Baker, but not to Matt Braunger. To everyone who ever had me on their podcast, especially Jimmy Pardo and Matt Belknap. To Betsy, Susy, Burke, Cady,

Caroline, Tommy, Danny, Chip, Mary Kate, and Libby for making our family even better. To Ben Wise and Junior for moving into my heart and immediately getting busy on renovations:

Thank you.

ABOUT THE AUTHOR

DAVE HOLMES is a writer-at-large for Esquire.com, an on-air personality at SiriusXM, a host of the *International Waters* podcast and the live game show *The Friday Forty,* and a guy who is on television sometimes. You can follow him on Twitter at @daveholmes if you're into that kind of thing, but he totally gets it if you're not. He lives in Los Angeles and sometimes New York and he can't believe you're actually reading this.